CAMPFIRE SMART COOKBOOK

Easy to Make Desserts for Campfire Cooking

(A Camping Cookbook That Novice Can Cook)

Bridget Carroll

Published by Alex Howard

© **Bridget Carroll**

All Rights Reserved

Campfire Smart Cookbook: Easy to Make Desserts for Campfire Cooking (A Camping Cookbook That Novice Can Cook)

ISBN 978-1-990169-43-4

All rights reserved. No part of this guide may be reproduced in any form without permission in writing from the publisher except in the case of brief quotations embodied in critical articles or reviews.

Legal & Disclaimer

The information contained in this book is not designed to replace or take the place of any form of medicine or professional medical advice. The information in this book has been provided for educational and entertainment purposes only.

The information contained in this book has been compiled from sources deemed reliable, and it is accurate to the best of the Author's knowledge; however, the Author cannot guarantee its accuracy and validity and cannot be held liable for any errors or omissions. Changes are periodically made to this book. You must consult your doctor or get professional medical advice before using any of the suggested remedies, techniques, or information in this book.

Table of contents

PART 1 1

COOKING OUTDOORS 2

PLAN AHEAD 3

EQUIPMENT 4

YOUR STOVE 4

POTS AND PANS 5

DISHES 5

FAST MEALS 6

- Beans & Sausage 6
- Creamed Chicken With Mashed Potatoes 7
- Salisbury Steak With Mashed Potatoes 8
- Roasted Chicken Salad With French Bread 9
- Creamed Ham & Eggs With Instant Rice 10
- Stir Fried Vegetables With Rice 11

BREAKFASTS 12

LIGHT AND PORTABLE BREAKFASTS 12

- More Substantial Breakfasts 13

INDIVIDUAL OMELETS WITH TORTILLAS 13

- Breakfast Burgers 14
- Cinnamon-Raisin Oatmeal 15

BIGGER BREAKFASTS 16

PANCAKES AND SAUSAGE 16

- Scrambled Eggs, Sausage Gravy And Fried Potatoes 17

LUNCHES 18

COLD CUT SANDWICHES 18

DELUXE BEAN BURRITOS	18
EGG SALAD SANDWICHES	19
TUNA SALAD SANDWICHES	19
ALMOST HUMMUS DIP	20
KITCHEN SINK PASTA SALAD	21

DINNERS **23**

BAKED POTATOES **24**

BEEF & BEAN BURRITOS	25
CABBAGE & NOODLES	26
CREAMY COLE SLAW	27
FIREPIT SQUASH	28
GIA'S BEAN SALAD	29
HOBO DINNER	30
RADICAL RADIATORE	31
ROASTED CORN	33
ROASTED SWEET POTATOES	33
SOFT TACOS	33
SPAGHETTI & SAUCE	34
STOVETOP SWISS STEAK	35
TUNA & NOODLES	36
TINFOIL CHEESY BREAD	37

DESSERTS AND SWEETS **40**

BANANA BOATS	40
COOKIES	41
CRAZY CAKE	41
EASY CHEESECAKE CUPS	43
FRIED APPLE TACOS	44
PEACH FRITTERS	45
S'MORES	47
CAFÉ AU LAIT MIX	49
HOT COCOA MIX	50
RICH HOT COCOA MIX	52
SPICED TEA MIX	53

BANDAGES **53**

BEE STINGS	53
BUGS	54
CELL PHONES	54
CAMPFIRES	55
CAMPGROUND COURTESY	55
CAMP STOVES	56
CORD	57
DISHES	57
FLASHLIGHTS	58
FIREWOOD	58
GARBAGE BAGS	58
GROUND CLOTH	59
JAMS AND JELLIES	59
OILS	59
NEW TENTS	60
PANCAKE SYRUP	60
PETS	60
RAIN	62
SEASONINGS	62
SEVERE STORMS	63
SUNBURNS	63
TARP	63
TENT STAKES	64
TODDLER RESTRAINT	64
TOILET PAPER	65
TOYS	65

PART 2 66

DELICIOUS AND EASY RECIPES 67

FOUR WAYS TO COOK 67

BARBECUING 69

- PICKING THE RIGHT CAMPING BARBECUE 70
- LUMP CHARCOAL VS. BRIQUETTES 71
- GETTING THE BARBECUE READY 73
- DIRECT AND INDIRECT GRILLING 73

BARBECUE RECIPES 74

- BACON-WRAPPED BARBECUE SHRIMP 75
- BARBECUED BABY BACK RIBS 76
- BARBECUE BEEF BRISKET 78
- BARBECUE BEEF RIBS 80
- BEER (OR SODA) CAN CHICKEN 82
- BISON BURGERS 84
- BOURBON BARBECUE CHICKEN WINGS 86
- CAJUN GRILLED SHRIMP 88
- CHILI-LIME GRILLED SALMON 90
- FILIPINO PORK SKEWER 92
- GRILLED PINEAPPLE 94
- GRILLED SQUASH 96
- GRILLED TURKEY 98
- HONEY DIJON CHICKEN BREASTS 100
- MEATBALL KABOBS 102
- SAUSAGE CORN KABOBS 104
- STEAK KABOBS 106
- STUFFED MUSHROOMS 108
- SWEET N' SMOKY BARBECUE SAUCE 110
- CHOOSING FIREWOOD 112
- MAKING A CAMPFIRE 113

CAMPFIRE COOKING RECIPES 115

- APPLE CIDER BARBECUE PORK CHOPS 115
- BACON-WRAPPED DRUMSTICKS 117

Brown Bag Breakfast Bacon And Eggs	119
Beef Skewers	121
Bannock Bread	123
Blueberry Pancakes	125
Campfire Quesadilla	127
Dad's Quick And Easy Tri Tip	129
Easy Beer-Battered Fish Fillets	131
Easy Omelets	133
Foil-Wrapped Baked Potatoes	135
Foil-Wrapped Cheesy Potatoes	136
Foil-Wrapped Ground Beef Veggie Stew	138
Foil-Wrapped Lemon Garlic Fish	140
Foil-Wrapped Popcorn	142
Foil-Wrapped Rainbow Trout	143
Foil-Wrapped Zucchini	144
Garlic Thyme Game Hens	145
Grilled Oysters	146
Grilled Turkey Drumsticks	147
Simple Grilled Rib Eye	148
Skewer Croissant Dogs	149
Stuffed Jalapenos	150
Roasted Potatoes	151
Rotisserie Leg Of Lamb	152
Sausage And Cheese Skewers	154
Tandoori Chicken	155
Veggie Foil Wraps	157
Seasoning A Dutch Oven	161
Temperature Control	162

DUTCH OVEN RECIPES 165

Barbecue Beans	166
Beef Stew	167
Blueberry Cinnamon Rolls	168
Cinnamon Apple Crisp	170
Cheesy Bacon Rolls	171
Chicken Fajitas	172

Chili Con Carne	173
Caramel Apple Pie	175
Cola Chicken	177
Cornbread	178
Corn Chowder	179
Easy "Sourdough" Bread	180
Egg And Sausage Casserole	182
Fried Eggs	184
Ground Beef Goulash	185
Meatloaf	186
Onion Rings	187
Pesto Chicken	188
Pizza Rolls	190
Pot Roast	191

Part 1

Cooking Outdoors

I know from practical experience that anything you can cook at home, you can cook outdoors.

Well, maybe almost everything. I don't think I would attempt soufflés or angel food cake while camping or on an open hearth.

I have, however, cooked almost anything else imaginable while camping. That includes cakes, cookies, yeast breads, quick breads and even cinnamon rolls.

I've cooked on open fires, propane, and charcoal out of doors. I've used cast iron, sticks, rocks, pots, and pans. I learned long ago that the typical campfire built by most campers is utterly useless for cooking too, unless you are just roasting hot dogs and marshmallows. Cooking fires are smaller, more easily managed, and often depend on coals to provide steady heat.

I have long assumed the role of camp cook when camping with a group. I'll confess, it's partly out of self-defense. I know I am a good cook, whether in the woods or in a kitchen. The same thing cannot be said for everyone else. I could either live on burgers and chips or I could just take over the cooking position. I happen to regard cooking as a challenge, not unlike a sport, and cooking outdoors often becomes the "extreme" version of the sport of cooking.

For years, I was also a single mom who was camping with her kids. That meant that I needed to do everything from setting up the tent to preparing meals and it included being the designated "activity coordinator". I couldn't go fishing, hiking, swimming or walk nature trails if I was enslaved to the camp kitchen.

I remembered that from my own childhood. Mothers often get the short end of the stick when it comes to camping. Somehow, moms have to pack everything from personal hygiene to safety gear, load it, unload it, help set up camp, and then prepare all of the meals and wash the dishes too. It's no wonder that many moms are less than enthusiastic about camping—they have the same chores as they do at home, plus they are made much more difficult by forcing them to do them with makeshift equipment!

But it doesn't have to be a case of enslavement to the camp kitchen. While it does require effort in advance, it is sometimes possible to actually recruit the rest of the family to help prepare and assemble the ingredients that will mean easy meals later.

Plan Ahead

Planning ahead is critical. The first step to planning is establishing exactly how long you will be camping. Most families camp for a weekend, which means arriving at their campsite on Friday afternoon or evening, and departing on Sunday afternoon to return home for the work week.

Using this as our example, we'll start planning what meals we need to have.

Friday means a simple and relatively quick dinner after the hurry of departing home and then arriving and setting up camp. Saturday has breakfast, lunch, and dinner. Sunday means a breakfast, and a simple lunch that can be easily prepared while camp is being taken down and packed away.

Remember, all recipes tell you how to adjust for the number of servings, as well as for adjusting servings for the amount a particular person will eat. Children eat much less than adults, and adolescents often eat more than adults. Leftovers are usually an undesirable result while camping, so are to be avoided by not preparing excess quantities of food.

Don't forget snacks either. It's amazing how hungry everyone becomes when they are engaged outdoors—it's as though everything tastes better too! While chips, packaged cookies, candies, and other commercially prepared treats are easy, for many families, they deliver too many calories, too much fat, and too much sodium to be considered healthy treats. Using fruits and vegetables as the base, there are other alternatives too.

Include one or two "emergency" options that are shelf stable. Sometimes, things happen. Your departure may be delayed, a meal may be lost, forgotten, or damaged somehow. Freeze dried meals and canned foods are excellent options for this. If nothing goes wrong, the same "emergency meals" will be used all summer long as your backup plan, finally being used on the last trip of the year or as a meal at home.

To make your planning easier, recipes are broken down according to the niche that they are used. Remember, these niches are not set in stone! You may use these recipes in any grouping that you choose.

Equipment

Your Stove

A stove is almost essential, unless you are content eating all cold or raw foods. Many areas do not allow open fires, have fire restrictions often, or there is not enough fuel to depend on an open fire. While cooking on a campfire may have a lot of romance and ambiance, it lacks in practicality.

Camp stoves are usually easy to use, and can be bought for about $20 for a simple single burner stove that uses butane or propane. Two burner stoves make cooking about as easy as cooking at home. Other, more expensive models, may include legs or even an oven.

No matter what model you use, be familiar with the stove, its operation, and its owner's manual. Bring along enough fuel to last for the entire trip.

Pots And Pans

Next to your stove, this is the most important gear you can bring. Non-stick pots and pans make clean up easier. Cast iron, while they are great to use and are the traditional camping pans, are very heavy to carry and difficult to pack.

Read your recipes, and be familiar with which pans will be needed. Most recipes can be accomplished with a large, deep skillet, an 8 quart dutch oven, and a 4 quart saucepan. Coffee drinkers will want to add either a stovetop percolator or a small tea kettle and a drip container to hold their filter and coffee for dripping. A medium mixing bowl, mixing spoon, slotted spoon, spatula, ladle or large spoon, and knife will round out your essentials. A large, sturdy baking sheet can also be useful as a portable countertop that is easily cleaned (and more sanitary than a picnic table.)

Washing up needs to be done just like at home. Rather than using an actual sink, a dishpan or large bowl can do the job. Hot water heated in a pan or tea kettle on the stove is mixed with cold water to make warm dish water. Dishes are then rinsed in clean cold water. In addition to the container, a pail for carrying water from a spigot, a dish cloth, nylon scrubber, dish soap, and a dish towel for drying dishes are all necessary items.

Dishes

For each person, bring one plate, bowl, cup/mug, spoon, knife, and fork. Making everyone responsible for washing their own dishes works for some families, while others rotate dish duty among everyone except the cook.

Fast Meals

These meals are designed for quick preparation. That means using canned foods, pre-cooked foods, and more convenience foods than most meals. None of them will take more than thirty minutes to go from taking out of the food box to dividing portions among your starving campers. Most will take even less.

Beans & Sausage

(10 minutes)

1 lb. fully cooked smoked sausage

1 lg. can baked beans

Cut sausage into 1" thick slices and package at home for easy preparation in camp.

Heat skillet over medium high heat. Add sausage and brown slightly while turning often. (about 5-10 minutes) Open beans and pour over sausages. Continue cooking, stirring occasionally, until beans are bubbly and hot. (about 4-5 minutes) Makes 4 servings.

Creamed Chicken With Mashed Potatoes

(15 minutes)

2 c. cooked chicken, cut into bite size pieces (rotisserie chicken works well)

1 pkg. country gravy mix (to make 2 c. gravy)

1 can peas, drained

1 pkg. complete instant mashed potatoes (to make 2 c. mashed potatoes)

Water

Prepare mashed potatoes according to package directions. Cover and set aside.

Make gravy according to package directions. Add chicken and peas, and continue cooking over medium heat until heated through. Serve by ladling gravy over mashed potatoes on plate or in bowl. Makes 4 generous servings.

Stretching it: This recipe can be "stretched" by doubling the amount of gravy while using the same amount of chicken and peas. Double the amount of mashed potatoes.

Salisbury Steak With Mashed Potatoes

(20 minutes)

1 or 2 frozen hamburger patties per person

2 pkgs. Brown or mushroom gravy mix (makes 1 c. gravy per package) Use 1 pkg. of gravy for 2 hamburger patties.

2 onions (adjust to ½ onion per hamburger patty) sliced or chopped

1 pkg. complete instant mashed potatoes (use more pkgs. if necessary, calculating 1/2 -1 c. of prepared mash potatoes per person)

water

Place hamburger patties in skillet and place over medium high heat. Cook hamburger patties through, turning halfway. (About 8-10 minutes.) Remove patties from pan and set aside. Pour onions into skillet and cook until soft and translucent.

Measure out water for gravy. In a small cup or bowl, combine gravy mix with ¼ c. water per package. Add remaining water to onions in skillet to begin heating. Stir in gravy mix and bring to a boil, stirring constantly. (About 3-4 minutes) When mixture boils, return hamburger patties to gravy, ensuring all patties are covered in gravy. Cover and set aside.

Prepare instant mashed potatoes as directed on package.

Serve on plate or in shallow bowl with gravy and patty served over potatoes.

Roasted Chicken Salad With French Bread

(5 minutes)

This is courtesy of a deli, either on route or near your destination as you want the chicken to still be warm.

1 rotisserie chicken

1 bag mixed salad greens

1 bottle salad dressing (ranch or Italian works well or use your favorite)

1 loaf fresh French bread

Divide greens among plates. Drizzle on salad dressing and top with pieces of chicken pulled from bones with a fork. Cut or break chunks of French bread to accompany salad.

Creamed Ham & Eggs With Instant Rice

(10 minutes)

Prepackage the measured rice in a container or bag. Prepare the ham and eggs and package them in a bag or container. Keep cold until meal is prepared.

1 pkg. country gravy mix (to make 2 c. gravy) prepared according to pkg. directions

1 c. diced ham

4 hard-boiled eggs, peeled & chopped

1 tsp. prepared mustard

3 c. instant white rice

3 c. boiling water

Pour boiling water over instant rice. Cover and set aside to rehydrate.

Make gravy according to package directions with water. When gravy is done, add ham, eggs, and mustard. Continue cooking 1-2 minutes to heat ham & eggs thoroughly.

Serve over rice. Makes 6 servings.

Stir Fried Vegetables With Rice

(15 minutes)

Prepackage measured rice in bag or container. Purchase prepackaged vegetables at the store, keeping the stir fry mixture frozen until departure.

1 (16 oz.) pkg. frozen stir fry vegetables

1 (16 oz.) pkg. cole slaw mix cabbage

¼ c. soy sauce

2 tbsp. vegetable oil

3 c. instant rice

3 c. boiling water

Mix boiling water with instant rice. Cover and set aside to rehydrate.

Heat oil in large, deep skillet. Add stir fry vegetables and cabbage. Cook over medium high heat, stirring often, until vegetables are done. (8-10 minutes) Add soy sauce and stir again.

Serve vegetables over rice, adding soy sauce to taste.

Makes 6 servings.

Breakfasts

Breakfasts while camping can range from fast & light to more substantial and time consuming to prepare. The reason for the variety is that the amount of time that is available to devote to the breakfast depends on a lot of variables, ranging from whether or not your crew is made up of early risers or whether you have early activities planned. The meal also varies according to individual preferences. Some people both need and enjoy breakfasts, while others prefer something light and portable. Many of the light and portable breakfasts can be taken along as "just in case" options.

Light And Portable Breakfasts

Breakfast bars

Granola bars

Nutrition bars

Granola, packaged in single serving size in sandwich bags

Trail mix in single serving bags

Peanuts, packaged in single servings in sandwich bags

Peanut butter on bread or tortillas

Fresh fruit

Boiled and peeled eggs, wrapped in plastic wrap and chilled

More Substantial Breakfasts

These breakfasts are more substantial, yet still quick and easy to prepare.

Individual Omelets With Tortillas

Tortillas travel much better than loaf bread due to their flat shape. They also wrap around things in a convenient manner, turning many foods into finger friendly foods.

These omelets are perfect for "do it yourself" breakfasts with minimal clean up. The individual bags can be pre-assembled at home as well. If pre-packaging these omelets at home, always use quart sized freezer bags and then place the prepared bags inside of either a gallon sized freezer bag or a large plastic storage container to prevent leaks from damaging other food in your cooler.

1 bag

2 eggs, cracked into bag

¼ c. shredded cheese

¼ c. crumbled cooked bacon OR diced ham

Vegetables can be added, but are best either pre-cooked or suitable to eat with little cooking

To prepare:

Bring water to a boil in a large saucepan. Squish closed bag with hands to mix ingredients evenly and combine yolks with whites. When water is boiling, drop sealed bag into water. Cook until eggs are firm, using tongs to fish bag out of water and lay on plate to cool slightly and then remove from bag.

Place cooked eggs into center of tortilla and roll tortilla around it, creating a finger-friendly package.

Breakfast Burgers

These take a bit more time, as well as leave the cook with a dirty skillet, but they are still portable and relatively quick to make.

The recipe that follows is directions for one sandwich. Multiply as needed.

1 precooked burger sized sausage patty (available in pork, turkey, and beef in the frozen food section)

1 slice cheese

1 egg

1 burger bun

Heat skillet over medium high heat. Heat sausage patty, browning each side. Place sausage patty on bun bottom and top with slice of cheese. In skillet, cook egg until firm through, scrambling or breaking yolk for speedier cooking. Place cooked egg on top of cheese, top with bun top and serve.

When cooking multiple breakfast burgers, it works best to cook eggs individually, using a small (8") skillet. With practice, it takes less than 1 minute per egg to cook it.

Possible variations include using ham instead of sausage. To skip cooking the meat at all, shaved deli ham can also be used.

Cinnamon-Raisin Oatmeal

This is a quick meal for even a fairly large group and very warming on a crisp, cold morning. The recipe is to make one substantial serving or two more moderate ones.

1 3/4 c. water

¼ c. raisins

½ tsp. cinnamon

¾ c. quick oatmeal

Measure water into saucepan. Add raisins and cinnamon. Bring mixture to a boil over high heat. Reduce heat to simmer, and cook raisins for about 10 minutes, or until they become plump looking.

Increase heat to medium high again, and stir in oatmeal. Cook for about 1 minute, stirring occasionally. Remove from heat and serve with sugar, brown sugar, and/or milk. Shelf stable ultra-pasteurized milk in 8 oz. boxes are convenient when camping for use with cereal, drinking, etc. It tastes best when chilled for 24 hours and served ice cold for drinking.

Variations can include:

Cinnamon apple: use diced fresh or dried apple instead of raisins. Fresh apple only needs 1-2 minutes of cooking.

Cherry: Use dried cherries and omit cinnamon.

Peach: use fresh or dried diced peaches. Cinnamon may be omitted, and fresh fruit needs little cooking.

Date-Nut: Use chopped dates plus 1/4 cup chopped nuts of your choice. Add dates & nuts with oatmeal, and reduce water by ¼ c.

Bigger Breakfasts

This is for the days when a substantial breakfast is served. These menus are more substantial, take more time, and dirty more dishes and pans than the others.

Pancakes And Sausage

This has to be a classic breakfast for camping. Using brown and serve or pre-cooked sausage, either in patty or link form, speeds up the process. After heating or cooking, keep them covered to retain their warmth. Calculate 4-8 links or 1-2 patties per person. Don't forget the syrup, but for less mess, jams and jellies can be a great alternative topping for pancakes. For that buttery flavor we all love, butter flavored syrups can be used. Another option is squeeze margarine or soft, tub margarine (if kept in cooler).

For your pancake batter, use a complete mix that requires no more preparation than just adding water. Bring along a bowl with a spout for easy mixing and dispensing. Using a non-stick skillet or griddle ensures success in cooking your pancakes, and do not try to cook them in the same skillet as your sausage—they **will** stick.

Pancake batter can be pre-packaged into a reclosable plastic bag or container, according to the number of servings you intend to cook. If using a new box of pancake mix, bring a reclosable bag to keep the extra from being spilled.

Scrambled Eggs, Sausage Gravy And Fried Potatoes

This is another classic big breakfast for camping. It will require three skillets, as well as plates for serving.

The following recipe will serve about four moderately hungry campers.

½ lb. crumbled cooked sausage (cook it at home and package it in a plastic bag)

1 pkg. country gravy mix (makes 2 cups gravy)

8 eggs

2 tbsp. margarine or butter

6 medium potatoes, scrubbed and cubed

1 onion, diced

½ tsp. salt

½ tsp. pepper

½ c. shortening (package it in foil or plastic)

water

Heat shortening in large skillet over medium high heat. Add potatoes, salt, and pepper. Cook, stirring occasionally, until potatoes are soft and beginning to brown, about 18-20 minutes. Add onion and reduce heat to medium and cook until onions are soft.

While potatoes are cooking, prepare gravy as directed on package. Add sausage and cook for 1-2 minutes longer to heat sausage through. Cover and set aside.

Melt butter in skillet over medium high heat. Crack eggs into skillet and stir with spatula to break yolks and combine with whites. Continue cooking and stirring until eggs congeal. Remove from heat.

To serve, top fried potatoes with sausage gravy and accompany with scrambled eggs.

Lunches

Lunches tend to be a grab and go meal, and it should be easy to prepare and eat. Sandwiches, salads and wraps are naturals for this light midday meal.

Cold Cut Sandwiches

Having an assortment of sliced bread or buns, cold cuts, sliced cheese, and condiments in squeeze bottles is an easy way to let everyone prepare their own midday meal. Using paper plates or a paper towel means that there are no dirty dishes makes it even easier.

It is important to keep these sandwich ingredients cold, as well as protecting them from contamination from the water of melting ice. While using reclosable freezer bags goes a long ways towards protecting your cold cuts, putting these bags inside of a plastic container with an airtight seal will improve your chances of preventing contamination.

Deluxe Bean Burritos

1 can refried beans

¼ c. sour cream

¼ c. minced onions

6 6" tortillas

Salsa or taco sauce

Place about ¼ c. beans in center of tortilla. Top with a tablespoon of sour cream and another of minced onion. Fold tortilla around beans. Serve with taco sauce or salsa.

Egg Salad Sandwiches

Egg salad is one of those quick things, and while some people prefer it chilled, others love it when it is made with still-hot boiled eggs and served warm. This is easy to make in camp, and can be multiplied to serve all of your campers.

4 slices bread

2 eggs

1 tbsp. mayonnaise

1 tsp. mustard

1 tbsp. sweet pickle relish

Dash of pepper

Place eggs in water to cover in small saucepan. Heat over medium high heat until water boils. Boil eggs for 9 minutes after the water reaches a rolling boil. Remove from heat and run cold water over eggs until just cool enough to handle. Peel eggs & rinse under cold water to remove any trace pieces of egg shell.

Place eggs in a small bowl. Mash roughly with a fork until no large pieces remain. Add remaining ingredients and stir to evenly combine. Divide between two slices of bread, top with a second slice, and cut sandwiches in half. Serve immediately.

Tuna Salad Sandwiches

2 cans tuna in water, drained

2 eggs, boiled & peeled

4 tbsp. sweet pickle relish

1 tbsp. finely minced onion

4 tbsp. mayonnaise

Place all ingredients in small bowl and mix with fork, breaking any large chunks of tuna apart. Spread on bread, rolls, or crackers, as desired.

Almost Hummus Dip

Prepare this at home one or two days before departure. Keep cold until serving.

3 cans garbanzo beans, drained & rinsed

1 jar roasted red pepper, drained & coarsely chopped

¼ c. extra virgin olive oil

4 cloves garlic, peeled & minced

1/3 c. lemon juice

1 can pitted black olives, drained

1 ¼ tsp. salt

½ tsp. ground black pepper

½ tsp. curry powder

½ tsp. ground coriander

½ tsp. ground cumin

½ tsp. oregano, crushed

1 tsp. lemon zest

1 small can chopped black olives

Put everything except the chopped black olives into a blender and puree until fairly smooth. Scrap ingredients into bowl, stir in chopped black olives. Refrigerate several hours or overnight tightly covered. Serve with crackers, flatbread, or pita chips.

Kitchen Sink Pasta Salad

This pasta salad is adaptable to your tastes and preferences, as well as very filling and tasty. It's easy to serve after being prepared at home and transported in a tightly sealed plastic container. It can also be pre-packaged into individual sized containers, if preferred. Keep it in the cooler until it is served.

1 lb. pasta, cooked according to package directions (shells, rotini, ziti, or whatever shape you desire)

1/2 c. mayonnaise

1/2 c. plain yogurt

1/2 tsp. salt

1/4 tsp. black pepper

1/4 tsp. lemon pepper

1 tbsp. cider vinegar

1 can whole kernel corn, drained

1 can green peas, drained OR 1 c. fresh or frozen peas

1/2 c. chopped celery

1/2 c. chopped red bell pepper

1/4 c. finely chopped onion

1/2 c. sliced or salad olives (black or green, use your favorite)

1/2 c. coarsely chopped pickles (sweet or dill or mild pickled peppers)

4 boiled eggs, peeled & coarsely chopped (optional)

1/2 c. crumbled bacon (optional)

1 c. shredded cheese (optional)

1 c. finely chopped ham (optional)

Combine mayonnaise, yogurt, salt, pepper, lemon pepper, and vinegar until smooth. Add corn celery, pepper, onion, olives, pickles, bacon, and ham. Stir to combine well. Add peas, eggs, and cheese, stirring gently to combine.

In large bowl, combine vegetable mixture with pasta, stirring gently to evenly mix ingredients.

Cover tightly and chill overnight for best flavor.

Peanut butter and jelly or honey sandwiches

This is a great solution to the sandwich issue. Honey requires no refrigeration, and most peanut butters also does not need refrigeration. In moderate weather, most jams and jellies will stay cool enough to prevent spoilage over a weekend. Squeeze containers of jams and jellies are also available, making preparation even easier.

Salads

Prewashed, prepackaged greens mixtures are easy to serve salad solutions. Remember to prevent contamination from melting ice—it can carry bacteria from other foods, resulting in cross contamination. Keeping foods in individual plastic containers that seal tightly helps reduce chances of this happening.

Salad dressings, in their bottles with snap or screw lids, are easy to take along. Try to bring only one or two different kinds.

Salads can have add-ons such as chopped veggies, shredded cheese, or diced cooked meat as well.

Dinners

Dinners are more substantial, but a typical weekend only includes one dinner. This is a time to have a bit of fun, more than devote yourself towards challenging preparation. None of these meals are going to consume much time to prepare, and some preparation may need to be done at home before your departure.

Choose recipes that suit your family's tastes and dietary preferences. Remember too, recipes are nothing more than guidelines, so feel free to experiment. Adding a favorite veggie, or eliminating one that is hated can go a long ways towards making a dish your own.

None of these recipes requires specialized cooking equipment, instead focusing on typical pots and pans, as well as aluminum foil.

To cook foil packets, use coals only. Having a blazing fire is going to result in burned food that is likely to also be undercooked inside. Mix and match dishes you find here for your gourmet camping best, and mixing foil packets with a dish cooked on your stove makes for an easy cooking experience.

Baked Potatoes

Scrub potatoes, pat dry, and rub with oil or shortening. Sprinkle with kosher salt and wrap in aluminum foil. Bake on coals for about 30-45 minutes or until tender. Serve with butter, sour cream (optional), salt and pepper. Additional toppings can include crumbled cooked bacon, hot chili with or without beans, cheese, shredded cheese, or diced ham.

Potatoes can be easily prepared at home and wrapped in foil. Place toppings inside small containers or bags inside of a tightly sealed plastic container in your cooler.

Beef & Bean Burritos

1 dozen burrito size tortillas

1 can chili with beans

1 can refried beans

1 lb. ground beef or turkey

1 pkg. taco seasoning

1 onion, chopped

½ c. water

Hot sauce or salsa, if desired

Brown ground beef in large skillet. Add onion and continue cooking, stirring occasionally, until onion is soft. Drain off fat from meat mixture, and stir in taco seasoning. Add water and cook, stirring often, over medium high heat until mixture comes to a boil. Add canned chili and refried beans, stirring to combine. Cook over medium high heat, stirring often, until mixture is bubbly, 3-4 minutes.

Spoon mixture into center of tortilla, folding tortilla around filling to make a burrito. Add hot sauce or salsa, as desired. Makes 12 generous burritos.

Cabbage & Noodles

Cut the cabbage at home, and put it in a plastic bag or container, transporting it in your cooler. Cook the dish just before serving.

1 medium. green cabbage, cored & cut into 2x1/2" strips

2 tsp. salt

5 tbsp. unsalted butter

1 tbsp. caraway seed

4 oz. wide egg noodles (about 2 ½ c.)

¼ c. sour cream, room temperature

Salt & Pepper, to taste

Heat water in 6 qt. dutch oven with salt. When it begins to boil, drop in noodles and cabbage. Cook as directed on noodle package (about 10 minutes usually.) Drain noodles and cabbage. Stir in butter and caraway seeds. Add sour cream and toss to combine. Season with salt and pepper to taste. Let stand 10-15 minutes to blend flavors before serving.

Creamy Cole Slaw

4 cups cabbage, shredded

1/2 cup carrots, shredded

3/4 cup mayonnaise

1/3 cup sour cream

1/4 cup sugar

2 tablespoons vinegar

3/4 teaspoon seasoning salt

1/2 teaspoon ground mustard

1/4 teaspoon celery seeds

Mix cabbage and carrots in a plastic bag. Chill.

In small bowl, mix remaining ingredients and pour into plastic container. Keep ice cold for up to 48 hours before combining with cabbage and serving.

Mix cabbage mixture with dressing well and chill about an hour before serving. Keep leftovers in cooler and use within 24 hours.

Firepit Squash

This is a fun one, and it is a little bit sweet, which appeals to those with a sweet tooth.

1 medium winter squash (buttercup squash works very well)

1 c. packed brown sugar

1 c. coarsely chopped raw bacon OR ¼ c. margarine or butter

Cut squash like a jack o lantern—by cutting around stem to make a lid. Make it almost as wide as the top of the squash, and leave an obvious notch to make it easy to replace lid for cooking and a tight fit. Scrape off any stringy material and seeds clinging to "lid" and set it aside. Remove all stringy material and seeds from interior of squash and discard. Do not add sugar and bacon or butter until just before baking, although squash can be cleaned and prepared before leaving home. Package brown sugar and bacon in small plastic bags. Make sure bacon is refrigerated until squash is cooked. Wrap squash loosely in aluminum foil, then in a bag to protect it until it is to be prepared.

To prepare squash: put sugar and bacon or butter into cavity. Replace lid and seal foil around squash. Cook on coals that are not too hot for about an hour or until the squash flesh is soft. To serve squash, scrape flesh away from skin and mix with sugary juices before removing from squash interior. Some may prefer to add some salt as well.

Adding spices such as cinnamon, nutmeg, and allspice can make this taste even more like dessert than a vegetable. These spices can be added with the sugar before baking.

Gia's Bean Salad

This is my own recipe for bean salad, and it makes a substantial quantity, suitable for serving a crowd. It also keeps well, as long as it is kept cold. For camping, it is prepared at home, and in camp, it's merely a case of serving the already prepared salad, making it quick and easy.

1 c. red wine vinegar

1/2 c. sugar

2 tbsp. honey

1/4 c. olive oil

1/2 tsp. salt

1/4 tsp. black pepper

1 tsp. dry mustard

1 tsp. garlic powder

2 tbsp. Greek seasoning

1 tsp. celery seed

1 29 oz. can garbanzo beans, drained and rinsed

1 29 oz. can black beans, drained and rinsed

2 regular size cans cut green beans, drained

1 regular size can kidney beans, drained and rinsed

1 medium onion, quartered and thinly sliced

Combine vinegar, sugar, honey, oil, salt, pepper, mustard, garlic, Greek seasoning, and celery seed in bowl, whisk to combine well. Add beans and onion, toss to combine. Refrigerate overnight to let flavors combine. Makes about 15 servings.

Hobo Dinner

This recipe gives the ingredients for one foil packet, which is sufficient for the average camper. Those who prefer heartier meals may want another one. For very young children, making smaller packets is also an option to consider.

Don't try to skimp on the foil—it will leak if you do. Instead of merely pinching seams together, roll or fold the foil over together to create a tighter seal. A tight seal will ensure that the foil packet does not leak and allow it to stay moist and flavorful.

1 potato, sliced

½ onion, sliced

1 stalk celery, cut into 1" pieces

1 carrot, sliced

1 raw hamburger patty

1 tsp. flour

1 tsp. salt

½ tsp. pepper

1 tsp. garlic powder

1 tsp. Worcestershire sauce

Take a foil rectangle, about 18" long usually, and set it on a flat surface. Put about half of the potato in the center and top with about half of the other vegetables. (There is no need to be exact.) Top with Worcestershire sauce and then hamburger patty. Put seasonings and flour on top of patty, then add remaining vegetables, ending with potato slices.

Fold and seal inside of foil. Keep on ice until they are cooked.

To cook foil packets: Have scattered coals (2-3" between each) that are moderately hot. Bake 20-30 minutes on each side, being careful to not puncture packets when turning. Let stand off of fire for about 10 minutes before serving to help reduce steam burns when opening hot packets.

Radical Radiatore

This dish is partially prepared at home, including cooking the pasta, and then is merely finished in camp. It can be made the day before departure, and then served on the second evening in camp. This eliminates the need to bring along a colander to drain the pasta, or the need to even cook the pasta. It is reheated by adding it to the boiling hot sauce. As a meatless dish, it's economical, but it can be served with meats such as ground beef, Italian sausage, smoked sausage or ground beef.

Radiatore has been used because it is a sturdy pasta, and it is designed to grab as much sauce as possible, making it very flavorful. The nugget-type pasta is also easy to eat and can be served in a bowl & eaten with a spoon, ideal for the younger crowd.

16 oz. radiatore pasta, cooked according to package directions, drained and tossed with 2 tbsp. olive oil. When cool, package in plastic container with airtight lid and refrigerate.

1 jar or can spaghetti sauce (any flavor)

1 c. diced bell pepper

1 c. diced onion

2 c. diced or sliced summer squash (yellow or zucchini)

1 c. sliced mushrooms

½ c. diced celery

1 c. shredded carrots

1 tbsp. minced garlic

1 tbsp. fennel seed

1 tsp. rosemary

¼ c. olive oil

1 c. shredded mozzarella cheese

½ lb. cooked crumbled or sliced meat (optional)

Grated parmesan cheese (top sprinkling, optional)

Package the vegetables, fennel seed, and rosemary together in bag or container, tightly sealed. Keep refrigerated until ready to cook.

Heat oil in a large, deep non-stick skillet. Add vegetable mixture and cook over medium high heat for 10 minutes, stirring often. Add spaghetti sauce, cover, and reduce heat to medium, stirring often. When mixture comes to a boil, reduce heat to simmer, and cook 15-20 minutes or until veggies are all tender. Stir in pre-cooked pasta and continue to cook with lid on for 5 minutes. Stir in shredded cheese and cooked meat, if desired. Remove from heat and let stand for five minutes before serving.

Variations: Garden-style: Use your favorite veggies. Eggplant is a natural to add, as are fresh tomatoes. Fresh herbs, such as basil, will also enhance the dish.

Pizzaria Style: Add sliced pepperoni that has been coarsely chopped, along with more cheese and sliced olives.

To serve: This dish is easily served in bowls and can be eaten with a fork or a spoon. Garnish each dish with some parmesan cheese and enjoy!

Roasted Corn

Peel husks back, but do not tear off. Rub off silk and replace husks. Wrap in foil. Roast over hot coals for 10-20 minutes (it depends on what kind of wood or charcoal it is, how hot it is, etc.) turning every 2-4 minutes to roast evenly. Properly roasted corn should have some areas that are golden brown, some scorched husks, but the kernels should not be "milky" when pressed with a fingernail or knife. Squeeze margarine, salt, and pepper make excellent accompaniments.

Ears of corn can be prepared at home before departure, including wrapping with foil.

Roasted Sweet Potatoes

Wash 1 sweet potato per person. Pat dry and wrap in aluminum foil. Bake over coals until it is squeezable soft (use an oven mitt to test it—it will be hot.)

Serve hot, warm or cold—depending on tastes. Butter, sour cream, salt & pepper, or a dusting of cinnamon are all popular toppings. I happen to like mine hot with cinnamon or plain and cold. (They taste sweeter when cold.)

To bake on coals: have moderately hot coals, scattered 2-3 inches apart. It takes 30-60 minutes, depending on the size of the sweet potatoes and temperature.

Soft Tacos

This will make a good dozen tacos and typically serve 4-6 people.

1 lb. ground beef

16 oz. angel hair shredded cabbage

1 onion, minced

1 can diced tomatoes

1 pkg. taco seasoning

8 oz. shredded mild cheddar cheese (or your favorite)

12 soft taco size tortillas

Sour cream (optional)

Taco sauce (optional)

Over medium high heat, crumble ground beef into skillet. Add onion, and cook until onion is soft, stirring often. Add shredded cabbage and continue cooking for 5 minutes, stirring often. Stir in taco seasoning and evenly combine with cabbage mixture. Add tomatoes to mixture, and bring to a boil, stirring frequently. Continue to cook until mixture thickens slightly, 1-2 minutes. Remove from heat.

Spread about $1/12^{th}$ of mixture into each tortilla. Sprinkle with cheese. Top with sour cream and taco sauce, if desired. Fold & eat!

Spaghetti & Sauce

This is another shelf stable ingredient dish, although fresh veggies and/or meat will also make the dish more flavorful.

1 can spaghetti sauce (your choice of flavor & style)

1 (16 oz.) thin spaghetti or angel hair

Grated parmesan cheese

Cook spaghetti according to package directions. While spaghetti is cooking, heat sauce. Drain spaghetti. Top spaghetti with sauce, sprinkle with parmesan cheese, and serve. Makes 4-6 servings.

Variations: Diced raw veggies, such as mushrooms, bell pepper, summer squash, and eggplant are naturals to sauté in a bit of olive oil, and then pour the sauce on top to heat it. Italian sausage, ground beef, or ground pork can also be cooked (or pre-cooked) and added to the sauce. Link sausages should be sliced into ¼" thick slices before being added to the sauce for getting the most mileage out of the least amount of meat.

Stovetop Swiss Steak

This probably never came from Switzerland, but it is based on a dish my mother used to make in the oven that was called Swiss steak. It's a bit slower cooking, but requires minimal attention once the initial preparation has been made. Doing the prep work at home keeps it easy to assemble and cook in camp.

2 lbs. (approximately) lean steak, about 1/2-1" thick, cut into individual serving size pieces (about 8 pieces)

8 potatoes, quartered

4 onions, peeled and quartered

2 cans diced tomatoes

1 tbsp. garlic

4 stalks celery, sliced

1 sm. can tomato paste

½ tsp. pepper

1 tsp. rosemary

1 tsp. beef bouillon granules

Pour tomatoes into dutch oven with a lid. Add garlic, rosemary, beef bouillon, and pepper. Stir to combine. Add meat, potatoes, onions, and celery. Cook over low heat for about 2 hours or until ingredients are tender, stirring occasionally. Add tomato paste, and cook 10-15 minutes longer, stirring occasionally.

One serving will include 4 pieces of potato, 1 piece meat, and 2 pieces of onion, along with some sauce to top it. This recipe makes 8 servings.

Tuna & Noodles

This is a simple dish, and it uses shelf-stable items, making it a good "emergency" meal to take along just in case it is needed.

1 (16 oz.) pkg. egg noodles

2 cans water packed tuna, drained

1 can cream of mushroom or celery soup

1 can peas, drained

1 tsp. lemon pepper

Cook noodles as directed on package. Drain and immediately stir in tuna, peas, and lemon pepper. Serves 4-6.

Variations: Use chicken (canned or leftover rotisserie) instead of tuna for chicken & noodles. Canned soup can be cream of chicken, mushroom or celery.

Cheesy Tuna (or chicken) Add 1-2 cups shredded cheese to noodles with the other ingredients.

Tinfoil Cheesy Bread

While I know that "tin foil" is more properly called aluminum foil, many people do still commonly refer to this magical and useful stuff as "tin foil." Regardless whether you say tin or aluminum, it's the aluminum foil we are referring to in this case, and it will go a long ways towards making some very tasty cheesy bread. The bread is most easily prepared at home, wrapped in foil and then put on the coals to cook in your campsite.

1 loaf French bread

¼ c. olive oil

2 tbsp. minced garlic

½ tsp. salt

½ tsp. pepper

½ tsp. fresh rosemary, minced

¼ c. butter or margarine, softened

½ c. grated parmesan cheese

2 c. shredded mozzarella cheese

Heat olive oil in small skillet over medium heat. Add garlic, pepper, and rosemary. Cook for 3-4 minutes, stirring often, until garlic begins to soften and turn golden. Remove from heat and scrape mixture into small bowl to allow to start to cool. When mixture is just warm, stir in softened butter and salt, stirring to blend mixture. Add parmesan cheese and mix well.

With a serrated knife, split the French bread lengthwise. Spreading it open like a giant hot dog bun, spread butter mixture over both surfaces of the loaf. Layer shredded mozzarella cheese over bottom half and then close bun.

Place filled loaf on a large piece of aluminum foil. Very carefully cutting to prevent cutting foil, cut loaf into 1 ½-2" thick slices. Fold foil over bread, folding it together to seal tightly lengthwise first, and then the ends. Keep loaf relatively cool until ready to prepare.

To prepare cheesy bread: Spread a thin layer of coals (3-5" between coals) the length of the loaf. Lay foil wrapped loaf over coals and turn every 2-3 minutes, heating for about 10 minutes total.

Snacks

Snacks are an important part of camping, but that does not mean that you are restricted to high sodium & fat options such as potato chips and dip. Any finger food that does not require preparation just before consuming can become a snack food.

Preparing snacks at home prior to departure and packaging them in single serving size portions may seem a lot of work, but for those who want to stick to a healthy diet, it can help ensure that no one overindulges. One standard healthy snack is raw veggies with dips. This is a great choice, and dips and dressings for these can be packaged in small plastic containers that hold a single portion. Using low-fat recipes will help keep the calories down, and one easy way to do that is to use non-fat yogurt to replace sour cream without losing the desirable creamy texture in standard recipes or with mixes. Vinaigrettes are another option for adding a flavor punch to veggies without adding a lot of calories.

Fruit is another healthy snack option, especially fresh fruit. Preparing fruit in advance for easy eating can help some families eat more of it, while others prefer eating the fruit out of hand. Use fruits that your family is fond of, chilling cut fruit, and keep whole fresh fruit cool and out of the sun.

Canned fruit is also available in single serving packages and is also another option. Dried fruit can be packaged in snack sized bags for easy distribution.

Cheese and Crackers

Cheese and crackers makes an easy snack that is particularly filling after physical exertion. Bring 2-3 different kinds of crackers, along with sliced cheese.

Peanut butter & crackers

Easy to prepare with relatively shelf stable foods, peanut butter and crackers is a great high protein snack. Pair your favorite brand of peanut butter with different kinds of crackers for variety, such as bacon flavored, buttery crackers, saltines, graham, etc.

Popcorn

Leaving the microwave at home may initially be somewhat daunting when it comes to popcorn, but long before technology came along, people were popping popcorn. Campsite solutions includes stovetop poppers, as well as Jiffy Pop.

Jiffy Pop delighted children long ago (yes, I'm older than the heyday of the air popper) and still can deliver the same delight at watching the foil expand with the popcorn's popping today.

Popping corn also delivers entertainment in other stovetop poppers, making it far more fun than pre-popped corn in bags. Not many snacks are as much fun as popping corn.

Stuffed Celery

Stuffed celery is one treat that many people enjoy and it is easily prepared in camp. Celery is prepared at home by washing it and cutting it into sections 3-4" long, reserving the leafy ends for another purpose. To stuff the celery, simply spread the cavity in the piece with peanut butter, cream cheese, or processed American cheese spread.

Desserts And Sweets

Don't forget that those with a sweet tooth will have it along on your camping trip. Neglecting it can lead to complaints and whining too! In addition, certain sweets have a long association with the idea of camping, and there are those who believe that no camping trip is complete without at least one of them.

Here are some options to help you avoid the candy bars, commercially baked cookies and cakes, and the whining for a trip to the ice cream parlor.

Banana Boats

These are easy to make, tasty, and probably have some sort of nutritional contribution to make as well.

1 firm banana

1 tbsp. (more or less) chocolate chips

6-12 mini-marshmallows

Lay the banana on its "back" so that it curves upward. Using a paring knife, cut a V-shaped section out of the top and carefully remove it, leaving the skin attached. Set the banana flesh aside (or eat it now.)

Distribute the mini-marshmallows and chocolate chips through the banana and fold the skin back down over the cut out section. Wrap in aluminum foil.

Cook slowly with just a few coals, keeping the banana on its back. The goal is to heat it thoroughly and melt the chocolate and marshmallow without scorching the banana.

To eat: Open the foil carefully and peel back the skin flap. Scoop the flesh out, along with the melted marshmallow and chocolate, with a spoon, taking care to avoid burns.

Cookies

Cookies are a delicious addition to any camping trip and a nearly ideal dessert too. While commercial offerings are delicious, nothing can taste better than homemade ones. Homemade cookies can be transported in a sturdy plastic container with an airtight lid to keep them fresh.

Crazy Cake

This cake is sized down for a smaller family. It's a not-too-sweet cake that is sturdy enough to survive camping trips. Bake it at home the day before departure, then for easiest serving, wrap each slice with plastic wrap before placing it into a larger container. Instead of frosting, sprinkle the hot cake with about ¾ c. chocolate chips. Let stand for a minute or two, and spread chocolate into a thin layer over the top of the cake. Let cake cool, cutting into squares before the chocolate sets. After cutting into squares, chill cake in freezer or refrigerator to set chocolate. Wrap tightly, and keep moderately cool until eaten to prevent chocolate from melting.

1 cup all-purpose flour

2/3 cup white sugar

1/4 teaspoon salt

3/4 teaspoon baking soda

2 tablespoons and 2 teaspoons unsweetened cocoa powder

1/4 cup vegetable oil

2 teaspoons distilled white vinegar

3/4 teaspoon vanilla extract

2/3 cup cold water

Preheat oven to 350 degrees F.

Sift flour, sugar, salt, soda, and cocoa together into a ungreased brownie pan (7.5"x11"). Make three wells. Pour oil into one well, vinegar into second, and vanilla into third well. Pour cold water over all, and stir well with fork.

Bake at 350 degrees F for 20-30 minutes, or until tooth pick inserted comes out clean. Let cool to room temperature before cutting into squares.

Easy Cheesecake Cups

These are tasty, easy to prepare and pack, and delicious. The hard part will be protecting them from predatory forks in advance of the meal they have been prepared for.

1 pkg. vanilla instant pudding

1 pkg. lemon instant pudding

2 (8 oz.) pkg. cream cheese

2 c. ice cold milk

8 small (1-2 c.) plastic containers with tight fitting lids

8 graham crackers

1 can cherry or blueberry pie filling (optional)

Beat cream cheese until fluffy. Beat in pudding mixes until evenly combined, and then slowly beat in ice cold milk. Immediately divide between the 8 containers. Cover and refrigerate. Transport & store in cooler until served.

To serve: Crumble 1 graham cracker on top of the cheesecake inside the container. Add a spoonful or two of pie filling, if desired.

Fried Apple Tacos

This one is a bit more work than most of the desserts, and some people enjoy these for breakfast too. They do require two pans—one for cooking the apples and one for the pancakes that form the taco shell in this case. The apples can be cooked ahead and reheated, although they aren't quite as tasty that way.

Cook the apples first, and keep them warm, then assemble the tacos as the pancakes are cooked. Make them as large (or small) to suit the diner.

Pancake mix, made as directed for 8 pancakes

2 tsp. cinnamon, divided

1 tsp. nutmeg, divided

1 tbsp. flour

½ c. brown sugar

¼ c. butter or margarine

4 apples, cored & cut into bite size pieces (shape doesn't matter!)

Put apples, half of the cinnamon, half of the nutmeg, brown sugar, and flour in plastic bag. Shake to evenly distribute ingredients. Set aside.

Stir half of the cinnamon & nutmeg into the pancake mix. Set aside.

In saucepan or skillet, heat butter over medium high heat. Sprinkle apple mixture into skillet and continue cooking, stirring occasionally, for 15-20 minutes or until apples are tender. Set aside and cover to keep warm.

Cook pancakes in desired size. Most adults will find 4-6" appropriately sized, while young children may prefer 2-3" diameter pancakes for their apple tacos. To assemble the apple taco, simply place 1-2 spoonfuls of the apple filling in the center of the pancake and fold in half. Eat while still warm.

Peach Fritters

This is something that I have often been asked to make in camp and has become a running joke with those who have camped with me often. They are easy, delicious when warm, and delight both young and old.

It's also rare that I specify a particular brand of anything, but after trying other brands and discovering why other people couldn't duplicate the fritters at home, I discovered that the key ingredient was a particular brand of complete pancake mix: Krusteaz. None of the other name brands or the generic brands I have tried have produced the fritters correctly. Deep frying over a camp stove is somewhat daunting, but it isn't hard. It also keeps the mess and oily smell out of your house.

2 c. pancake mix

1 egg

1 can peach slices in juice

1 tsp. cinnamon

Sugar for dusting over fritters (may be omitted)

Using a sharp knife, run knife through peaches in can to randomly cut them into small pieces. Put pancake mix into mixing bowl and stir in cinnamon. Add egg and peaches in juice. Stir to combine. Mixture should be thick and sticky, so that when you pick up a spoonful, you have to push it off of the spoon. If mixture is too thin, add more pancake mix. If it is too thick, add some milk or water.

Heat skillet or dutch oven over medium high heat, with 2-3" deep oil until hot enough to brown a cube of bread in about 30 seconds. Drop peach fritter batter into hot oil in 1 tsp. sized lumps. Lift out with slotted spoon and drain off grease on brown paper or paper towels. Dust warm fritters with sugar, if desired. These taste best while warm, and this recipe will serve 4-12 people, depending on how hungry they are! Coffee, tea, or hot cocoa go well with them too.

Roasted (or Toasted) Marshmallows

Roasting marshmallows over a campfire is an iconic camping activity. That does not mean you should not put some thought into it. Not all campgrounds are going to have sticks suitable for roasting marshmallows. In addition, if you are not proficient in identifying young trees, it is possible that a poisonous species could be accidentally used. It's easier to bring "sticks" from home. A variety of roasting forks are available, made with metal and stay-cool handles.

The fire should be hot, but not with blazing flames dancing high. Soft woods such as pine give off a lot of soot, which will tend to coat marshmallows (and everything else) with black soot that is not only visually unappealing, but does not taste particularly good either. Hard woods work much better, as does charcoal.

To toast marshmallows like a pro, insert the end of your roasting fork into one of the flat ends of the marshmallow. Hold it about 12-18" from the coals, slowly turning it as it begins to bubble and turn brown.

Remember that these are VERY hot when removed from the fire and must be handled with care. Some roasters prefer to remove the roasted "skin" portion of the marshmallow and eat that first, then either eat the soft center portion or re-roast it again.

For a gourmet treat, try making homemade marshmallows to roast.

S'mores

This is a classic camping dessert and almost everyone loves them, despite the fact that they are messy. They are simple to assemble, wrap and heat on your campfire, but the real payoff of eating them is usually the messiest part. Have your wet wipes ready to manage sticky fingers and faces!

This is to make one s'more.

2 graham crackers

2 marshmallows

½ plain chocolate bar

Aluminum foil square

Lay one graham cracker in the center of the foil. Break chocolate bar in half, placing one half on each side of the graham cracker, then topping it with a marshmallow. Put the second graham cracker on top, then seal foil around s'more with folds.

Heat over coals for 3-5 minutes to melt marshmallows & chocolate. Remove from heat and let stand for 3-4 minutes to cool off somewhat. Unfold carefully and enjoy.

Beverages

Camping beverages include a lot more than canned sodas and bottled drinks. These recipes include easy to transport mixes, as well as ideas for managing beverages such as milk and baby formula.

For cold beverages, keep them in a different cooler than your other food items. This helps reduce cross-contamination from food items to beverages. It also reduces the frequency in which ice will need replaced, as the beverage cooler is accessed much more often than food coolers are. Always keep your cooler in the shade, and a damp towel over the top will help keep the exterior cool as well.

Gallon sized water bottles, kept cool, can refill re-usable water bottles at a far lower cost than individual water bottles. To flavor water, there are a number of liquid and powdered flavorings available that offer flavor without sugar.

Individual fruit juices are convenient solutions to serving juice in camp with minimal mess. These are available in a variety of packages from bottles to pouches.

Baby Formula

Powdered formula, mixed as needed, is obviously the easiest way to bring along baby's preferred beverage. Premixed formula needs to be kept in the cooler and surrounded by ice. Screw down lids help reduce chances of contamination from melting ice.

Café Au Lait Mix

1 1/2 c. instant non-dairy creamer (such as Coffeemate®)

1/4 c. brown sugar (packed)

1/4 c. instant coffee

dash of salt

Combine ingredients well. Store mix in air tight container.

To use: Combine 1/4 c. mix with about 2/3 c. boiling water and stir.

Carbonated Beverages

These come in convenient single serving cans, are sweet, and not expensive either. However, many people believe that these beverages are very bad for health and well-being. Despite this, many families that normally avoid them consider them a treat that they indulge in while camping.

Keep the cans out of direct sunlight, and immerse in ice for several hours before serving for best results. Remember that the sweetness that attracts humans also attracts insects and animals alike. Cover cans if they are being sipped slowly to prevent a bee (or some other insect) from crawling into the can, only to sting lips or mouth when someone takes a drink. Don't forget to dispose of empty cans appropriately as well. Most campgrounds have a collection point for recyclables such as aluminum cans.

Hot Cocoa Mix

10 cups dry milk powder

4 3/4 cups sifted confectioners' sugar

1 3/4 cups unsweetened cocoa powder

1 3/4 cups powdered non-dairy creamer

In a large mixing bowl, combine milk powder, confectioner's sugar, cocoa powder, and creamer. Stir till thoroughly combined. Store cocoa mixture in an airtight container. Makes about 15 cups mix, or enough for about 45 servings.

For 1 serving, place 1/4 cup cocoa mixture in a coffee cup or mug, and add 3/4 cup boiling water. Stir to dissolve. Top with a few marshmallows, if desired.

Milk

Taking milk along camping can be difficult. One of the easier solutions is shelf stable ultra-pasteurized milk. It is available in both single serving and quart sized containers. For best flavor, chill for 24 hours before serving and shake well. Always use before the expiration date.

For cooking purposes, powdered and canned (evaporated, not sweetened condensed) milk is a convenient solution that is also economical.

Dry milk comes in different forms. Some is non-fat, and some is whole fat. Non-fat milk keeps longer and has larger granules. Nido, packaged by Nestle, is an instant milk. It mixes quicker and more closely resembles fresh milk. It is sold in cans with resealable plastic lids and is very convenient. Mixed with room temperature water and then chilled for 12 hours, few people are going to notice the difference after they pour it on cereal or even in their glass. If the flavor is noticed, strawberry or chocolate flavor syrup is likely to conceal it.

Soy and Almond milk is typically sold in cartons. For best results at taking these milks along, repackaged them into plastic bottles or jars with screw down lids. Keep bottles upright to prevent leaking or contamination from melting ice.

Fresh milk usually is sold in plastic bottles in the United States. These containers just need to be kept upright in the cooler to prevent leaking or contamination from melting ice.

Rich Hot Cocoa Mix

2 c. Nestle's "Nido" instant whole milk

1/4 c. Hershey's Special Dark cocoa

1 c. unsweetened cocoa

1/2 c. granulated sugar

1 c. powdered sugar

1 c. powdered non-dairy creamer

Combine all ingredients in a 1 gallon ziplock bag and shake until evenly mixed. Store cocoa mix in an airtight container. For each serving, use about 1/4 c. cocoa mix with 12-14 oz. very hot water. Stir until dissolved. (If it tastes "watery", it means you need another spoonful or two of mix added to the hot water

Spiced Tea Mix

2 c. orange drink mix (the kind with sugar)

1/2 c. lemonade mix (the kind with sugar)

1/2 c. instant tea (unsweetened)

2 tsp. cinnamon

1 tsp. ground cloves

1/4 tsp. allspice

Mix all ingredients evenly. Store mixture in airtight container.

To use: Put 1-2 tbsp. in mug and add boiling water.

Camping Hacks
Here is your secret chapter that will help you become the mega-expert that everyone turns to for camping problem answers. None of it is rocket science, and not all of these hacks are going to be things that everyone will use. Pick the ones that apply to you and your family.

Bandages

Minor scrapes and cuts often need a bandage to cover them. The usual plastic bandages are not going to stay adhered to skin well, and will fall off often. Using fabric bandages will ensure they stay where you stick them longer. Make sure to pat skin dry after cleaning wound and using alcohol to clean skin before adhering the bandage will help it stick longer.

Bee Stings

When bee stings occur, remember to scrape the stinger off rather than pinching it (like with tweezers) to remove it. The tiny stinger also has a tiny bag of venom attached, and squeezing this tiny bag will force more venom into the sting. Items such as butter knives or even credit cards work well to scrape across the sting and remove the stinger.

A traditional remedy for stings is to make a paste of baking soda and water and apply it to the affected area. Including a box of baking soda with your camping gear is a good idea.

Bugs

The Great Outdoors is home to bugs as well as plants and cute furry animals, and unfortunately, many of the bugs find humans quite tasty. Don't forget insect repellant. For after the bite, there are a number of remedies sold. Hydro cortisone cream is also great for taking the itch out and encouraging healing. If necessary to prevent young fingers from scratching until it turns into an open wound, cover bites with bandages and call them their war wounds!

Cell Phones

We all love our cell phones, and they provide a great service very conveniently. I sometimes wonder how we ever survived without one.

At the same time, part of the charm of going camping is disconnecting from the normal world we live in. If everyone's nose is buried into their phone, they are not gaining much benefit from their outdoor experience.

That means some kind of balance is needed. Setting limits, for both adults and children, will keep the cell phones available for emergencies and the family engaged with the outdoors, even reluctant teens. Turning all cell phones to airplane mode, for example, between breakfast and dinner, keeps the cell phone out of the way during the bulk of the day.

Keeping cell phones protected from weather and activity related casualties can also be important. Dry bags and containers are sold to fit most cell phones to allow them to remain accessible.

Campfires

Campfires are not essential for camping, and are not an efficient or easy way to cook meals either. Despite this, most campers enjoy the ambiance of sitting around a camp fire. In campgrounds, these fires are usually restricted to a fire ring.

Starting the firewood on fire does not require rocket fuel or gasoline. In fact, neither one works very well for starting a fire and present a number of dangers.

For safer fire starting, charcoal lighter fluid can be used. A more traditional method would involve using kindling (small pieces of wood) One efficient method is to wrap a few pinecones with a sheet of newspaper, twisting it tightly on the ends. Small twigs, more pinecones, and shavings would be arranged on top of this. Light the end of the twisted paper, adding dry grass or shredded paper to encourage the flames to grow. When the smaller pieces catch the flame, slowly add larger pieces, until the fire is large enough and hot enough to ignite a split piece of firewood. Burning two or three pieces of wood at a time is all that is needed to keep the fire going, adding one as the flames die down into coals. During an evening of sitting by the campfire, one or two bundles of wood will usually be burned. If you intend to cook foil packets on the fire, adding a dozen or so charcoal briquettes will start to burn and last longer, allowing for food to be cooked over coals. (Charcoal can be transported from home or bought ahead.)

Campground Courtesy

Observe campground courtesy yourself and teach your children to observe it as well. This includes obeying campground rules as well as a few additional items. While some of these may seem as though they should be understood by everyone, they aren't. Children often need to be actually told and taught that these things are not to be done.

Don't take short cuts through other occupied campsites.

Don't touch, disturb, snoop through, or take things from other campsites.

Don't let your pet disturb others.

Don't tease other people's pets to get them to bark or otherwise react.

Don't play games or use toys too close to other campsites. Examples are playing with Frisbees or balls that end up landing in other campsites. Take them to an open area to use.

Don't shine your flashlight deliberately at other people's tents or into their campsites unless searching for a lost child or pet.

Don't play loud music or other sounds loud enough to disturb others, even outside of quiet hours. (Certain hours are regarded as "quiet" in most campgrounds, typically from 10 pm to 8 am.)

Don't tempt others by leaving expensive equipment or toys unattended and in plain view.

Keep your campsite neat.

Don't feed the animals, no matter how small and cute they are.

Smile and be friendly and courteous to other campers. It's free!

Don't make a mess in communal areas such as restrooms, shower rooms, or laundry areas. Clean up after yourself if it does happen.

Camp Stoves

There are hundreds of kinds of camp stoves. Some burn alcohol, kerosene, butane, propane, white gas, or gasoline. For most purposes, butane or propane are the simplest to operate and often the least expensive. Car camping stoves range in price from about $20 to about $200, depending on the size and type. Using a propane or butane stove is nearly identical to using your stove at home. Always read and be familiar with your stove's owner's manual.

Propane is sold in one pound canisters as well as in larger sized containers such as are used for barbecues. Camp stoves will typically need a converter to use the larger containers. Gauging the amount of fuel necessary for a weekend is an important skill that only comes with practice. Running out of fuel is a good way to have a very bad weekend, so to always carry a spare canister is a good idea. Initially, bringing four canisters should provide more than enough fuel for the most active camp cook.

Have stick matches, as well as a long barbecue lighter, available for lighting your stove, even if it comes equipped with an integrated lighter.

Cord

Cord comes in a wide variety of sizes and strengths, as well as materials. Probably the most useful is what is typically called paracord or 550 nylon paracord. It is strong, thin, lightweight, compact, comes in multiple colors and it is also incredibly useful. It can replace a broken belt for your pants, attach to a tarp or rainfly and a stake on the ground, become a clothesline or even support a hammock.

Dishes

By allotting each camper one set of dishes (bowl, plate, knife, fork, & spoon) and requiring that each person wash and put away their own dishes, it helps reduce the amount of work one person must do. Even the very young children can wash their own dishes with supervision.

Rotate pot & pan clean up as well, letting everyone take a turn cleaning up after meal preparation has been completed. While portable sinks are marketed for camping, an easy solution is a large bowl or dishpan.

Flashlights

Children love flashlights, but batteries don't seem to love children. To prevent buying enough batteries each weekend to supply a whole troop of adults, invest in shake or crank flashlights for each child. Two weekends of camping will more than pay for the investment.

In addition to the children's flashlights, each adult should also have a battery operated flashlight. Micro lanterns, typically using AA batteries, work well for illuminating tents, dining tables, and cooking areas. At least one per tent should be on hand. Keeping all flashlights, spare batteries, and lanterns together for easy access upon arrival at the campground is a good idea. Putting them in a pouch, small duffle bag, or small tool box can help accomplish that.

Firewood

Once upon a time, families either collected firewood at their campsite or brought it from home. Today, neither solution is advised. Campgrounds face too much pressure to allow collecting wood, and transporting firewood now transports insects and diseases, and is outlawed in many areas.

Today, firewood is typically purchased either at the campground or at a nearby store. Call and check on availability and restrictions before departure to allow for planning your purchase.

Garbage Bags

Most campgrounds are going to supply trash cans, complete with liners, but it is surprising how useful some garbage bags can be when camping. Here are some unintended purposes large garbage bags can be used for.

Tent bag for wet tent

Impromptu rain poncho—just cut or tear holes for the head and arms

Laundry bag

Table cover

Weather protection

Rescuing bedding from leaking tent

Bed wetting protection-put it under a blanket or sheet and over the sleeping bag

Protecting car from sandy, dirty or muddy feet and other items

Seat cover after swimming

Ground Cloth

Using a ground cloth under your tent will keep it cleaner as well as dryer. Small twigs and stones can also damage tent floors, and a ground cloth will help protect the floor.

Economy tarps or sheet plastic can be cut down to size, or folded back. Ground clothes should NOT extend beyond the edges of the tent, but should end 1 or 2" under the tent.

Jams And Jellies

Jam and jelly make great toppings for French toast and pancakes, as well as the classic accompaniment to peanut butter in peanut butter sandwiches. Some brands are available in squeeze bottles, making their use even easier, as there is no temptation for the shorter crowd to insert a spoon that was just dropped into the dirt.

Oils

Oils, whether for drizzling or for cooking, can be tricky and prone to leaking. If only a small amount is needed, such as 1-2 oz., an ideal way to bring them along is in a used drink mix bottle such as Mio is sold in. Pop off the top, rinse the container thoroughly, and allow to air dry for at least 24 hours with the top off. Use a marker designed for marking on plastic and label the contents. Not only does the container work well for a small amount of anything, but it delivers the contents with single drop precision.

New Tents

Always set up your new tent once at home. This ensures that if there is a defect, it is discovered before your camping trip. Even for experienced campers, practice in setting up a new tent is wise as well.

Seal all seams on a new tent with seam sealer. This ensures that there won't be surprise leaks appear the first time it rains.

Pancake Syrup

This is a sticky topic, and one no one wants to discover has been leaking all over everything in your food box. When it comes time to eat your pancakes, we also are not thrilled to discover that Junior used it all. One simple solution is putting single servings of syrup into a container, and doling out one container per person.

Used beverage mix containers, like those found with Mio and other brands is the simple and environmentally friendly solution. Pop off the top of an empty container, rinse it thoroughly, and air dry for 24 hours before using. Each container will hold 1-2 ounces, depending on the brand of drink mix, sufficient for one meal. Label containers with the contents using a marker designed for marking on plastic to prevent it from rubbing off. Many families may want to put the diner's name on as well to prevent disputes, especially with children.

Pets

Whether it is Fido, Fifi or Fluffy, we love our pets and we love spending time with them. Taking our pets along requires some planning and preparation.

First, make sure pets are allowed in the campground (most do.) Find out what special rules there are. Typically, it requires your pet to be quiet, kept on a leash no longer than 6' long, to not be left in camp unattended and for all waste to be picked up and disposed of properly. To obey all of these rules means that you will need to indulge only in activities which your pet can join the rest of the family. For activities that the dog or cat cannot join the family, it means a responsible adult must remain behind with the pet. Some families will opt to leave their pet at home rather than have a babysitter at camp for those activities.

Bringing along a crate can help confine your pet at night or at any other time when having them on leash is inappropriate. Remember to bring your pet's vaccination record (some parks will require you to show them) food, and their containers for food and water. It is also important to ensure that your pet remains physically comfortable and does not overheat or get too cold.

Preventing your pet from becoming lost or injured is important. Make sure that the collar is sturdy, that there is an ID tag with a valid telephone number (preferably your cell phone number)and the leash is also in good condition. Microchips can also help identify your pet, but the first line of identification is always an id tag and collar.

Any dog that may become aggressive with strangers or is nervous with strangers should also wear a muzzle for their own protection when in public areas such as a campground, as children often approach without warning. Soft muzzles are comfortable for the dog and also allow them to drink water while they are wearing it. Never leave your pet unattended in the campground, whether it is on leash or in a crate, as it is invariably against the rules and escapes can also occur. If your dog does escape without your presence, they are apt to become afraid and disoriented, and quickly become lost.

Rain

It is inevitable. Sooner or later, you will get rain while camping. If you have sealed your seams and done your annual re-waterproofing of your rain fly, everything in the tent should be fine. Then, the problem becomes how to occupy both adults and children during a rain storm.

If it isn't too severe, the best course is usually to continue with planned activities and add a rain poncho or rain coat to the attire. When the conditions drive everyone into the tent, it's time for an alternate activity. One compact activity is playing cards. There are card games of all kinds, and suitable for all ages over about age two or three. Packing along a deck or two takes little space and is a great low-tech way to engage the whole family. Dice games and dominoes are other choices.

Without any extra gear, there are verbal games that can be played such as the familiar "I'm going on a trip and I'm taking…" Storytelling is another way to fill time and entertain each other.

When it comes time for meals and meal preparation, having a tarp or canopy along can make it a much more pleasant experience without rain diluting your gravy or making your sausage swim.

Seasonings

Taking along full sized containers of various seasonings isn't necessarily compact or efficient. Instead of taking the entire container, pre-measured quantities for specific dishes can be packaged inside a small piece of foil or plastic. Putting all of the ingredients inside a single container for a dish or meal can ensure that nothing is forgotten or missed when packaging.

Severe Storms

Unfortunately, Mother Nature is not always considerate about when storms arrive or how severe they will be. Some severe storms will mean it is necessary to cut short your trip. On occasion, a severe storm may also arrive without warning.

When severe weather does arrive, a thin fabric tent will not provide much protection. Taking cover in one's car is one option. Another is to seek refuge in the restroom or other campground building.

Always remember: camping gear is replaceable. Human life is not.

Sunburns

Nothing can ruin a camping trip faster than a sunburn. Not only is the one with the bright red skin suffering, but their misery infects the entire family. Prevention is the first course of action, using sun screens, hats, and clothing to block burning rays.

Having relief for the burn after the event is also a good idea. There are numerous commercial creams for relieving the pain and discomfort of a sunburn. For home remedies, my favorite is to carry a quart of aloe juice, the type sold for drinking, in the cooler. Brushing or wiping the cold liquid on the burn would provide relief. Other remedies include using vinegar and applying it liberally to the affected area.

Tarp

It's amazing how useful a tarp can be. It can provide both sun and wind protection, as well as be used to keep the rain off. Carrying along an 8x10' "economy" tarp means you have a compact tool that can do multiple tasks such as becoming a temporary canopy, becoming a supplemental rainfly over a leaking tent, or even be used to create a small shelter to change clothes.

Tent Stakes

All tents use tent stakes, but not all tent stakes are created equally. In addition, different terrain and conditions requires different stakes. Stakes can also be bent or broken by striking obstructions such as tree roots or rocks.

Bring along at least two full sets of stakes, in 2 different types. The thin, wire-like stakes sold with tents are among the least useful stakes. Instead of these, carry the plastic one and a set of the longer v-shaped metal ones. Having a few spares is always a good idea.

Package your stakes in bags with a drawstring, and don't forget to include a hammer or mallet to hammer them in.

Toddler Restraint

Toddlers, as any parent can tell you, can vanish in the blink of an eye. While this is risky enough at home and while shopping, it can quickly turn bad when camping and hiking. To prevent this, use a dog collar as a belt on the child (or harnesses designed for this) with the buckle in back. Attach a leash—retractable ones designed for large dogs work great when hiking. Another option is to tie snaps on both ends of a section of paracord, snapping one end around a parent's waist or arm, and the other end to the toddler's dog collar. This allows the parent to accomplish tasks such as setting up camp, preparing a meal, setting out snacks, or even take a breather with a cup of coffee without Junior disappearing into the brush. Remember that tying your children up (that's how many people will perceive this) is not a substitute for actual supervision—it is still necessary to pay attention! The cord or leash simply means that if your attention is directed elsewhere for a minute, including supervising older children, the toddler is not going to wander off.

Toilet Paper

Most campgrounds have a toilet of some kind, but toilet paper availability varies. Put a roll inside of a coffee can (or plastic container) and snap the lid on to help keep moisture out. It transports easily to and from the restroom in the can.

Toys

Face it, kids like their toys, and parents like their kids to be happy. At the same time, going camping means that no one is in their usual environment and the primary focus should be given to the location and its activities. In addition, expensive toys are subject to loss, theft, or damage while camping.

To minimize problems, restricting how many and which toys are taken along on a camping trip is important to maintain one's sanity. When beaches are included in the activities, bringing along a small pail, molding containers and a scoop or small shovel are good toys to bring. Inexpensive balls are another great choice. Some families like having one or two electronic toys along for entertaining children in the evenings.

To get the most out of the camping experience, families have to balance convenience with the outdoor experience that they have gone camping to discover.

Part 2

Delicious And Easy Recipes

When you come back from a long day of camping fun, you don't want to spend hours slaving away over a hot camp stove or barbecue. Most of the recipes in this book are designed to be quick and easy, while still providing the nutrients and calories you need to go about your daily business.

While most people think slapping a few burgers or pieces of chicken on the grill or cooking up some hot dogs are pretty much the limits to what you can cook while camping, this book provides you with a number of interesting and delicious recipes that go above and beyond what you'd expect from camp food. There's no reason for you to have to eat junk the entire trip just because you're camping.

From early morning breakfasts to late night dinners and desserts, The Camping Recipe Book has you covered. You'll find a number of recipes in this book that are sure to become family favorites. Camp cooking just got a heck of a lot more interesting.

Four Ways To Cook

There are 4 methods used to cook the recipes in this book:

- Barbecuing.
- Campfire grilling and campfire foil-wrapping.
- Dutch oven cooking.

Barbecuing is synonymous with camping and you'd be hard-pressed to find a campground where there aren't multiple barbecues going, with people from all walks of life grilling all sorts of meats and tasty treats. Charcoal barbecues are the most common barbecue type used while camping, but gas barbecues have been known to make an occasional appearance. The type of barbecue you bring is up to you, but since most people prefer to bring charcoal barbecues camping, the recipes in this book assume use of a charcoal barbecue.

If you're using a gas grill, don't worry. You'll still be able to cook the recipes in this book. You're just going to have to make a few adjustments to your cooking methods. One of the biggest adjustments is going to be indirect grilling with a gas grill. Instead of moving coals around to create an area that's free of coal, you can simply turn on one burner and leave the other burners unlit. Place your food over the unlit burner and close the lid.

Cooking using a campfire is the most primitive method, harkening back to the days of old where the pioneers that explored this great country had only one option when it came to cooking food—fire. There's something to be said about cooking using the same method the pioneers used when they first explored this great country and a number of delectable meals can be made using the campfire. The campfire recipes in this book call for a grill that can be stood up over the campfire or for the foods being cooked to be wrapped in aluminum foil and placed directly in the fire.

There's another campfire cooking method many campers haven't heard of—a Dutch oven, which is a large cast iron pot that is seasoned with vegetable oils before use. You put the items you want to cook in the Dutch oven and place it directly onto the coals of the campfire. It heats up and cooks whatever is inside of it. Dutch ovens take a little bit longer than the other methods of cooking camp food, but they open up a world of possibilities when it comes to the camp foods you can make with them. They aren't overly expensive and once you've used one, you're going to want to bring your Dutch oven along every time you camp.

There's a good bit of overlap when it comes to the cooking methods used while camping. Recipes that call for barbecuing can just as easily be grilled on a grill placed over a campfire. Foil-wrapped items can be placed in a campfire's hot embers or they can be placed on the hot coals of a barbecue. Items cooked on a skillet placed on a campfire grill can be cooked on a Dutch oven lid flipped upside down and placed over hot embers. This overlap allows you to pick and choose the methods of cooking that are most convenient to you.

The methods you use to cook the recipes in this book are up to you. Regardless of the method, the food you cook will be easy to make and tasty. After all, isn't that what camping is all about?

There's one item that can be used to cook camp food that I haven't included in any of the recipes in this book other than to help prep some of the ingredients. Most campers bring a camp stove along when they go camping and many of these campers rely on it heavily, especially when it comes time to cook breakfast or whip up a quick snack at lunch time.

I didn't include camp stove recipes because they tend to be run of the mill recipes that can be cooked anywhere. If you want ideas for recipes you can cook on your camp stove, you can find them in pretty much any recipe book you buy. Any recipe that can be cooked in a skillet, a pot or a saucepan can be made using a decent camp stove.

I'm not going to go as far as to say you shouldn't bring a camp stove along on your camping trips because it does have its uses, but I'll tell you this. Every meal you cook with a camp stove is a delicious meal you're missing out on that could have been cooked using one of the other methods.

Barbecuing

When I'm at home on a warm summer (or fall or spring, for that matter) afternoon, there's nothing I love more than cracking open a beer and firing up the grill to cook up a tasty dinner. A good barbecued meat paired with a simple salad and a hunk of bread or two is all I need to be blissfully happy. That is, until the kids start bickering over who gets the last piece of meat, ruining my blissful nirvana.

Entire courses are taught on the intricacies of barbecuing. Thousands of dollars can be spent learning the nuances of the barbecue grill while attending courses at such revered schools as the Harvard School of Grilling or the Yale Barbecue Academy. OK, I made up those two schools, but there is a Weber Academy that teaches barbecuing skills . . . and people do pay to attend courses to learn how to get the most from their Weber grill.

The good news is you don't have to spend any money other than the cost of this book to learn to use your barbecue to cook the recipes in this chapter. They're easy to make and most of them will have dinner on the table in no time at all.

Before you get started cooking, you're going to have to choose a grill and decide what type of briquettes or charcoal you want to use. Let's get to it.

Picking The Right Camping Barbecue

Decisions. Decisions. Decisions.

You're going to have to pick from a wide array of barbecues when you buy your first camping barbecue. That is, unless you already have a serviceable barbecue you can fit into the vehicle you plan on taking camping, in which case all you'll have to do is pack it up when it's time to go.

Assuming you don't already have a good barbecue, the first decision you're going to have to make is whether to buy a gas grill or a charcoal grill. From a purely traditionalist standpoint, a charcoal grill is the way to go because they're easy to bring with you and impart a delicious smoky taste to food cooked using one. Charcoal grills are inexpensive and will cost significantly less than a similar gas grill.

Gas barbecues tend to be large and unwieldy, so you probably aren't going to want to cart one around with you when you go camping. There are smaller propane grills available, which are a good choice if you're dead set against using charcoal.

The next decision you're going to have to come to is how big of a grill you need. You can find everything from a small grill that'll only hold a couple burgers or steaks to gigantic grills capable of cooking enough food to feed an entire campground. The little hibachis are fine for single campers, but cooking for a family on one can be an exercise in frustration. The biggest barbecues are usually trailer-mounted units and aren't a good choice unless you plan on camping out with huge groups of people and have a vehicle you can tow one with.

Don't let your eyes get bigger than your trunk space. While it would be nice to have a huge Weber on which you can barbecue entire meals, you aren't going to want to try to fit a Weber and all of your camping gear in a hatchback Civic. If you have a truck, you don't have to worry about space as much and can get a larger grill. When it comes to grill size, your best bet is to buy as big of a grill as you can afford and can reasonably expect to be able to pack into the vehicle you plan on taking camping.

For the recipes in this book, either a kettle grill or an open grill will suffice. If you want to cook large slabs of meat, you're going to want to go with a larger kettle grill because they reflect heat better off the curved lid and the flow of oxygen into the grill is easier to control.

If you're looking to barbecue smaller pieces of meat, the type of grill you get really isn't critical as long as you don't go too cheap. Spending a little extra to get a heavy duty grill with a thick enamel coating will ensure you have a grill able to withstand the rigors of camping. You don't want a grill that's going to rust the first time you're caught in a surprise rainstorm and forget to wipe it down. Look for a grill made of thick steel that feels sturdy when you pick it up. Don't worry too much about the weight. You're only going to be moving it from your vehicle to your campsite.

Lump Charcoal Vs. Briquettes

Spend enough time around those in the know when it comes to barbecuing and you'll hear plenty of arguments about which is better, lump charcoal or briquettes. It's one of the most hotly debated topics when it comes to barbecuing. When it comes to which is the better choice, there isn't a clear answer. They both have their pros and cons and it's largely a personal choice as to which of the two better fit your needs.

Briquettes are made from a mixture of materials compressed into a small lump. They can include a number of materials, including char, wood charcoal, limestone, starch, sawdust and borax, amongst other things. They're cheap, they light easily and they burn consistently, which allows you to more easily regulate heat. The downside is they emit chemicals when first lit and food cooked using briquettes can have a chemical taste to them if you put the food on the grill before the briquettes have a layer of white ash covering them.

Lump charcoal is the top choice of barbecue purists because it's charcoal in its purest form. It's created by burning wood with little oxygen present and lump charcoal isn't packed with the additives and fillers found in briquettes. It lights up quickly and burns extremely hot, but tends not to last as long as equal-sized briquettes. Quality can vary greatly from bag to bag, especially with the cheaper lump charcoal. You're going to have to spend more money on lump charcoal and may buy a bag only to find it's full of small pieces of charcoal instead of the large lumps you were hoping for. Lump charcoal also has a tendency to pop and spray out sparks as it burns. If you aren't careful, you could end up with little burn marks on your arms and tiny pieces of ash in your food.

For the recipes in this book, it's up to you which of the two you use. These recipes can just as easily be cooked using either lump charcoal or briquettes. If you're new to the world of barbecuing, briquettes are more forgiving and less expensive, so I'd suggest starting with them and then moving to lump charcoal as you gain experience. Or you can stick with the briquettes. A lot of experienced barbecuers have tried both and prefer them to lump charcoal. It's your call.

Getting The Barbecue Ready

There are a couple schools of thought when it comes to prepping a barbecue. Some people stack their coals in the barbecue, cover them in lighter fluid and toss a match on top, watching as the coals light up in a blazing inferno. Others like to forgo the lighter fluid, instead opting to use a method that doesn't add more chemicals to the mix.

The best way I've found to light both briquettes and lump charcoal is through use of a charcoal chimney, which is a canister into which you place your lumps of charcoal and light them evenly from the bottom up without having to add lighter fluid.

Here's a quick tutorial on how to use a charcoal chimney:

1. Place a few sheets of newspaper at the bottom of the chimney. Crumple it up so there are air pockets to help it ignite.
2. Place the charcoal into the chimney.
3. Light the newspaper at the bottom of the chimney. It works best if you ignite it in a couple different locations around the bottom.
4. Watch to make sure the coals catch fire and then let them burn. The coals that light first will touch off nearby coals and eventually all the coals in the chimney will be lit.
5. Let the charcoal chimney sit for 15 to 20 minutes to give the coals time to ignite. The coals are ready as soon as they have a fine coat of white ash over them.
6. Once the coals are ready, dump them into the barbecue. It's time to start cooking!

Direct And Indirect Grilling

Direct heat barbecuing is done by placing food on the grill directly over the hot coals. You have to closely monitor foods cooked this way because dripping fat can cause flare-ups that can burn food or cause it to cook unevenly.

Indirect grilling takes place when you move the coals to one side of the barbecue and place the food you're cooking on the other side, so it isn't directly above the coals. This method slowly cooks food and foods cooked this way can take an hour or two (or longer). The food is usually placed above a drip pan designed to catch grease that drips off of the food in order to prevent flare-ups.

A good rule of thumb is to cook anything that takes less than 30 minutes to cook over direct heat and anything that takes longer than 30 minutes over indirect heat. Another technique involve searing meat over direct heat for a few minutes to lock juices and flavor in and then switching it to indirect heat.

Barbecue Recipes

The recipes in this section are designed with a charcoal barbecue in mind. Most of the recipes can just as easily be cooked on a grill placed over the campfire, but cook time may vary. They can also be cooked using a gas grill. Again, the cook times may vary, so keep a close eye on your food.

The recipe will tell you what method of barbecuing to use, indirect or direct grilling. Regardless of the method, open flames should be avoided. A spray bottle can be used to knock flames down or you can simply move your meat to another area of the grill where there are no flames.

Bacon-Wrapped Barbecue Shrimp

Serving size:

8 to 10 servings

Cooking method:

Direct heat

Ingredients:

20 jumbo shrimp, peeled and deveined

20 pieces of bacon

½ cup barbecue sauce

Toothpicks

Directions:

1. Place toothpicks in water and let them soak for at least 20 minutes.
2. Wrap each shrimp with a slice of bacon and pin it in place with a toothpick.
3. Brush shrimp and bacon with barbecue sauce and place on grill over direct heat. The shrimp should be big enough so they won't fall through the grill. If not, they're going to have to be cooked on a skillet or the shrimp can be placed on a skewer.
4. Cook until bacon and shrimp are cooked all the way through. Continue basting with barbecue sauce as necessary.
5. Let cool for 5 minutes and brush the shrimp with warm barbecue sauce right before serving them.

Barbecued Baby Back Ribs

NOTE: This is one of the few recipes in this book that isn't quick. Baby back ribs taste best when slowly grilled over indirect heat.

Serving size:

6 to 8 servings

Grilling method:

Direct heat

Ingredients:

3 racks baby back ribs

3 lemons

1 cup barbecue sauce (the Sweet n' Smoky recipe included later in this chapter is great for this recipe)

Rub Ingredients:

3 tablespoons salt

2 tablespoons garlic powder

2 tablespoons onion powder

2 tablespoons paprika

2 tablespoons cumin

1 tablespoon brown sugar

1 teaspoon chili powder

1 teaspoon cayenne pepper

Directions:

1. Cut lemons in half and squeeze juice over the racks of ribs on both sides.
2. Combine rub ingredients and rub into the ribs.
3. Let sit for at least 30 minutes.
4. Prepare barbecue for cooking over direct heat.
5. Place ribs on grill with bone side down.
6. Place ribs on grill and cook over direct heat for 7 to 10 minutes on each side.
7. Switch to indirect heat and cook for 1 to 2 hours, or until ribs start to separate from the bones.
8. Right before ribs are done, brush them liberally with barbecue sauce and let them cook for an additional 10 to 15 minutes.
9. Let cool for 5 to 10 minutes.
10. Cut ribs and serve warm.

Barbecue Beef Brisket

NOTE: This recipe also takes a long time to cook, but I'm including it because it's absolutely delicious.

Serving size:

7 to 10 servings

Grilling method:

Indirect heat

Ingredients:

3 to 5 pounds beef brisket

2 tablespoons liquid smoke

2 tablespoons extra virgin olive oil

¼ cup salt

¼ cup cracked black pepper

1 cup Sweet n' Smoky Barbecue Sauce (the recipe is included later in this chapter)

Directions:

1. Rub liquid smoke, olive oil, salt and pepper into the brisket.
2. Place brisket in plastic bag and refrigerate or keep cool in ice chest overnight.
3. Prepare barbecue for indirect cooking.
4. Place brisket on the grill so it isn't directly over the coals. You want the temperature to be between 200 and 250 degrees F in the cooking area.
5. Place the lid on the barbecue and let brisket cook for 4 to 6 hours, or until a meat thermometer inserted into the brisket reads 185 degrees F. Add charcoal as necessary to keep the temperature of the cooking area in the desired range.
6. When brisket is done, let it sit for a half hour before cutting it.
7. Cut and serve with Sweet n' Smoky Barbecue Sauce to dip the brisket in.

Barbecue Beef Ribs

NOTE: I cheat a little with this recipe and use Sweet Baby Ray's Barbecue sauce instead of making my own. There's something about this sauce that's tough to beat on barbecue beef ribs. If you don't want to use store-bought sauce, you can make the bourbon barbecue sauce from the Bourbon Barbecue Chicken Wings recipe or the Sweet n' Smoky Barbecue sauce at the end of this chapter.

Serving size:

4 to 6 servings

Grilling method:

Direct heat

Ingredients:

1 rack of beef ribs

1 onion, chopped

2 tablespoons salt

2 teaspoons pepper

1 bottle Sweet Baby Ray's Barbecue Sauce

Directions:

1. Separate the ribs by cutting between each bone to create individual ribs.
2. Rub ribs with salt and pepper.
3. Prepare barbecue for direct grilling.
4. Grill ribs over direct heat for 10 to 12 minutes, or until they're sizzling hot and starting to char just a little.
5. Coat the ribs with generous amounts of barbecue sauce and cook for 5 more minutes, turning regularly.
6. Remove from grill and let cool for 5 minutes.
7. Serve hot.

Beer (Or Soda) Can Chicken

Serving size:

1 chicken

Grilling method:

Indirect heat

Ingredients:

1 chicken

1 can of beer (or soda)

¼ cup vegetable oil

3 tablespoons salt

1 tablespoon pepper

¼ cup dry spice rub

Directions:
1. Clean out inside of chicken. Wash chicken and pat dry.
2. Rub chicken with vegetable oil and then rub with salt, pepper and dry spice rub.
3. Open beer (or soda) can and get rid of ¼ of the contents of the can.
4. Slide the chicken onto the can, so that at least half of the can is inside the chicken.
5. Prepare your barbecue for cooking using indirect heat.
6. Place chicken on grill, so that it isn't over the coals. The can should be upright. You can use the chicken's legs to help balance it on the grill.
7. Place lid on barbecue and cook the chicken for 60 to 90 minutes, or until the chicken is cooked all the way through.
8. Remove chicken from grill and let sit for 15 minutes.
9. Carve and serve.

Bison Burgers

NOTE: You can substitute regular hamburger for the ground bison in this recipe. I chose to use bison because it's lean meat and tastes great.

Serving size:

10 burgers

Grilling method:

Direct heat

Ingredients:

3 pounds ground bison meat

½ onion, chopped

1 clove garlic, minced

3 tablespoons fresh sage

2 teaspoons salt

2 teaspoons pepper

1 tablespoon extra-virgin olive oil

10 hamburger buns

10 slices of cheese

10 tomatoes

10 pieces of lettuce

Directions:

1. Add the olive oil, onion and garlic to a saucepan and sauté until the onions turn translucent. You can do this by placing a small pan on the barbecue or you can do it on a camp stove.
2. Let the onions and garlic cool for 10 minutes.
3. Combine onions, garlic, ground bison meat, sage, salt and knead the ingredients together with your hands.
4. Make 10 bison burger patties out of the meat.
5. Grill the burgers over direct heat for at least 5 minutes on each side, or until as done as you want them.
6. When there's a couple minutes left, place a slice of cheese on each of the burgers to give it a chance to melt.
7. Build your burgers and serve warm.

Bourbon Barbecue Chicken Wings

NOTE: This recipe may seem a bit difficult to make while camping because of the large number of ingredients required for the bourbon barbecue sauce. You can speed things up and cut down on the stuff you have to pack by whipping up a batch of the bourbon barbecue sauce at home before you leave. Or you can buy a bottle of bourbon barbecue sauce and not have to make it at all. When I don't feel like making bourbon barbecue sauce, I use Jim Beam Spicy Bourbon Barbecue Sauce or KC Masterpiece Smoky Bourbon Sauce.

Serving size:

5 to 7 servings

Grilling method:

Direct heat

Ingredients:

6 pounds of chicken wings

1 tablespoon of extra virgin olive oil

Bourbon Barbecue Sauce Ingredients:

1 cup bourbon whiskey

2 cups ketchup

1 cup water

1 cup onion powder

½ cup brown sugar

¼ cup tomato paste

¼ cup molasses

2 tablespoons apple cider vinegar

2 teaspoons garlic powder

1 teaspoon hickory liquid smoke

1 teaspoon tabasco sauce

Directions:

1. Combine the bourbon and water in a saucepan and bring it to a boil. This can be done on the grill or using a camp stove.
2. Stir in the rest of the ingredients and let simmer for 15 minutes, or until the sauce thickens up.
3. Prepare grill for direct grilling.
4. Coat grill with olive oil.
5. Place wings on grill and cook for 10 to 15 minutes on each side with the cover on the barbecue.
6. Brush bourbon barbecue sauce on wings and cook for another couple minutes on each side, or until wings are done all the way through.
7. If you want, you can brush more sauce on the wings right before you serve them.

Cajun Grilled Shrimp

Serving size:

8 servings

Grilling method:

Direct heat

Ingredients:

3 pounds shrimp, peeled and deveined

3 tablespoons olive oil

1 tablespoon lemon juice

1 teaspoon dried thyme

1 teaspoon dried oregano

1 teaspoon paprika

½ teaspoon cayenne pepper

8 skewers

Directions:

1. Place skewers in water and soak for at least 20 minutes, so the skewers won't burn.
2. Combine Cajun oil blend ingredients in a plastic freezer bag and shake until blended.
3. Thread shrimp onto skewers.
4. Brush shrimp with Cajun oil blend.
5. Place on grill over direct heat.
6. Grill until shrimp are pink and slightly charred. This will take approximately 3 to 5 minutes on each side.
7. Serve warm.

Chili-Lime Grilled Salmon

Serving size:

8 servings

Grilling method:

Indirect heat

Ingredients:

8 salmon fillets

4 limes, cut in half

3 tablespoons butter, melted

½ teaspoon chili powder

½ teaspoon cumin

½ teaspoon garlic powder

A pinch of salt

Directions:
1. Prepare barbecue for cooking over indirect heat.
2. Squeeze the juice from 3 of the limes.
3. Combine lime juice, melted butter, chili powder, cumin and garlic powder in a small bowl and stir together.
4. Coat salmon filets with chili-lime mixture.
5. Place filets skin side down on grill, away from the coals.
6. Cook using indirect heat for 15 to 20 minutes.
7. When the salmon start to get flaky, flip it over for a couple minutes and let the meat cook until you have grill marks on the salmon.
8. Remove the filets from the grill and squeeze the remaining lime over the filets.
9. Let cool for 5 minutes and serve warm.

Filipino Pork Skewer

Serving size:

10 to 12 servings

Grilling method:

Direct heat.

Ingredients:

2 pounds pork filets

½ cup lemon-lime soda

¼ cup soy sauce

¼ cup banana catsup

2 cloves garlic, minced

2 tablespoons brown sugar

A pinch of salt

A pinch of black pepper

10 to 12 skewers

Directions:

1. Cut pork into 10 to 12 equal strips.
2. Combine all marinade ingredients in a plastic bag.
3. Place pork in marinade and let marinate for at least 6 hours. This can be done before you leave to go camping, so all you'll have to do is skewer the marinated pork and cook it while camping.
4. Place skewers in water and soak for at least 20 minutes. This will prevent the skewers from burning when you place them on the grill.
5. Place 1 pork strip on each skewer. Poke the skewer through the end of the pork strip, twist and poke the skewer through again.
6. Continue twisting and poking until the entire pork strip is on the skewer.
7. Prepare barbecue for direct grilling.

8. Cook skewers over direct heat for 15 to 20 minutes, or until pork is cooked all the way through.

Grilled Pineapple

Serving size:

6 to 10 servings

Grilling method:

Direct heat

Ingredients:

1 large pineapple

¼ cup extra virgin olive oil

½ cup honey

2 tablespoons butter

Directions:
1. Peel the pineapple, core it and cut it into 1" thick rings.
2. Melt the butter and add butter, honey and olive oil to a freezer bag.
3. Shake until blended.
4. Place pineapple in bag and let marinate. You can prepare the pineapple the night before your trip and place it in the freezer bag until you're ready to use it.
5. Prepare the grill and lightly oil the grate with olive oil.
6. Grill pineapple for 3 to 5 minutes over direct heat.
7. The pineapple is done when it has been cooked all the way through. Light grill marks are good, as long as you don't overcook the pineapple and burn it.
8. Let the pineapple cool for 5 to 10 minutes and serve warm.

Grilled Squash

Serving size:

10 servings

Grilling method:

Direct heat

Ingredients:

5 squash

½ cup virgin olive oil

1 tablespoon garlic powder

1 tablespoon dried paprika

Salt and pepper, to taste

Directions:

1. Cut squash into strips long enough that they won't fall into the coals when placed on the grill.
2. Combine olive oil, garlic powder and paprika in a small bowl and stir until incorporated.
3. Brush olive oil mixture onto the squash and place on grill.
4. Cook for 8 to 12 minutes on the first side.
5. Flip over and brush with more olive oil.
6. Let cook for an additional 5 to 8 minutes on the other side, or until the squash is cooked to your liking.
7. Season with salt and pepper and serve warm.

Grilled Turkey

NOTE: This recipe works best when cooked in a large kettle grill. It's not quick, but is an easy way to cook a turkey. I've done it while camping and have even cooked our Thanksgiving turkey this way a time or two.

Serving size:

1 turkey

Grilling method:

Indirect heat

Ingredients:

1 whole turkey (10 to 12 pounds is preferable), cleaned and patted dry

1 onion, diced

2 cloves garlic, chopped

½ cup salt

3 tablespoons pepper

½ cup extra virgin olive oil

Directions:

1. Make sure turkey is completely thawed before attempting to barbecue it.
2. Stuff the onion and the garlic into the turkey.
3. Prepare barbecue for cooking. Use at least 5 pounds of coals.
4. Combine oil, salt and pepper and brush it onto the outside of turkey.
5. Place turkey into a roasting pan and place the roasting pan on the grill.
6. Place lid on barbecue. Make sure you leave the vents open or the charcoal will go out.
7. Cook turkey for 1 to 3 hours. The turkey is done when a meat thermometer inserted deep into the turkey reads at least 165 degrees. Add briquettes at least once an hour to ensure

heat remains consistent. You can add wood chips to impart a smoky flavor to the turkey. Hickory, mesquite and cherry all work well.

8. Let turkey cool for 15 minutes.
9. Carve and serve.

Honey Dijon Chicken Breasts

Serving size:
8 pieces

Grilling method:
Indirect heat

Ingredients:
8 chicken breasts
1 tablespoon olive oil
½ cup Dijon mustard
½ cup honey
2 tablespoons lemon juice

Directions:
1. Lightly oil the grill, so the chicken won't stick to it.
2. Combine the mustard, honey and lemon juice in a small bowl and stir until incorporated.
3. Set aside ½ cup of sauce for basting.
4. Brush the chicken with the rest of the sauce.
5. Cook chicken over indirect heat for 15 minutes.
6. Rub a light coating of sauce onto the chicken and cook for another 15 minutes over indirect heat or until the chicken is done.
7. The chicken is done when there is no pink in the middle. A few char marks are fine, but be careful not to burn it.

Meatball Kabobs

Serving size:

8 servings

Grilling method:

Direct heat

Ingredients:

2 pounds hamburger

5 egg whites

¼ cup water

½ cup dried breadcrumbs

2 teaspoons cumin

1 tablespoon garlic powder

1 teaspoon salt

1 teaspoon pepper

8 skewers

Directions:

1. Combine all ingredients in a large bowl and mix together until incorporated.
2. Form into meatballs and place meatballs on skewers.
3. Prepare grill for direct grilling.
4. Place skewers on grill and cook for 10 to 15 minutes, or until meatballs are cooked all the way through.
5. Season with salt and pepper, to your liking.
6. Let cool for a few minutes and serve warm.

Sausage Corn Kabobs

Serving size:

8 servings

Grilling method:

Direct heat

Ingredients:

2 pounds sausage, cut into rounds

4 cobs of corn, shucked and broken in half

1 pound small red potatoes

1 stick butter

1 tablespoon Old Bay seasoning

½ teaspoon cayenne pepper, optional

1 tablespoon extra-virgin olive oil

8 skewers

Directions:

1. Boil potatoes for 10 minutes, or until soft. You can use your camp stove for this, as it's easier than trying to boil water on a grill.
2. Thread sausage, potatoes and corn onto skewers. The corn should be in the middle, bracketed by potatoes and sausage coins.
3. Melt butter and mix in Old Bay seasoning and cayenne pepper.
4. Prepare grill for direct grilling.
5. Brush butter seasoning blend onto the kabobs.
6. Lightly oil the grill and place the kabobs onto it directly over the coals.
7. Cook for 8 to 12 minutes, or until corn is seared to your liking. Brush occasionally with butter seasoning.
8. Let cool for 5 minutes and serve warm.

Steak Kabobs

NOTE: Prepare these steak kabobs the day before your camping trip and leave the steak marinating in the sauce until you're ready to cook them.

Serving size:

12 kabobs

Grilling method:

Direct heat

Ingredients:

3 pounds steak, cut into 1" cubes

3 bell peppers, cut into 2" pieces

1 pound fresh mushrooms

1 fresh pineapple, cubed

¼ cup brown sugar, packed

¼ cup white vinegar

¼ cup soy sauce

1 teaspoon lemon juice

1 teaspoon garlic powder

1 teaspoon seasoned salt

12 skewers

Directions:

1. Combine all of the sauce ingredients in a freezer bag and shake until blended. Save ¼ cup of the marinade for grilling.
2. Place steak in the bag with marinade let marinate for at least 6 hours. Keep it on ice until you're ready to cook it.
3. Prepare the grill for cooking.
4. Thread steak, peppers, mushrooms and pineapple onto the kabobs.
5. Brush with saved marinade.
6. Grill for 10 to 15 minutes or until steak is cooked all the way through. Baste with marinade every couple of minutes.
7. Let cool for 5 minutes and serve warm.

Stuffed Mushrooms

Serving size:

8 to 12 servings

Cooking method:

Direct grilling (on foil)

Ingredients:

24 large mushrooms

1 cup sausage, cooked and crumbled

½ cup extra virgin olive oil

1 package dry onion soup mix

3 tablespoons garlic powder

2 tablespoons parsley

2 tablespoons tabasco sauce

1 cup mozzarella cheese

Directions:
1. Cover grill with aluminum foil.
2. Combine a couple tablespoons of the olive oil, the dry onion soup mix, garlic powder, parsley and tabasco sauce in a bowl and stir together until thoroughly mixed.
3. Remove stems from mushrooms.
4. Spoon the filling into each of the mushrooms.
5. Cook the mushrooms on the grill for 15 minutes.
6. Add the mozzarella cheese and cook them for another 5 minutes, or until the cheese melts.
7. Let cool for 5 to 10 minutes and serve warm.

Sweet N' Smoky Barbecue Sauce

NOTE: This barbecue sauce is absolutely delicious and can be used on a number of different meats. I've tried it on chicken, pork ribs, steak and beef ribs and haven't been disappointed yet. It includes a lot of ingredients, so it's best to whip a batch up before you go camping and bring it along with you.

Serving size:

Makes 3 to 4 cups of sauce

Grilling method:

None

Ingredients:

1 cup tomato sauce

1 cup ketchup

½ cup apple cider vinegar

¼ cup molasses

¼ cup honey

2 teaspoons liquid smoke

3 tablespoons packed brown sugar

1 teaspoon garlic powder

1 teaspoon black pepper

1 teaspoon salt

½ teaspoon onion powder

¼ teaspoon cayenne pepper

¼ teaspoon ground cinnamon

Directions:

1. Mix all ingredients in a saucepan and bring to a rolling boil over medium heat.
2. Let the sauce cook until it thickens. This usually takes 20 to 30 minutes.
3. Refrigerate the sauce until you're ready to use it.

Campfire Cooking: Grilling, Foil Wrapping, Etc.

Campfires aren't just for sitting around while telling ghost stories. There are a variety of ways you can use your campfire to whip up easy and delicious foods.

Here are just some of the many ways you can use your campfire to cook food:

- **Campfire grilling.** Place a grill over your campfire and barbecue food on it.
- **Direct heat.** Food cooked over direct heat in a campfire is cooked directly over the hot coals or the fire.
- **Indirect heat.** Food cooked over indirect heat is placed on the grill so it isn't sitting directly over hot coals or the fire itself.
- **Skewer cooking.** Find something thin enough to poke food onto and long enough to where you can hold it over the fire without getting burnt and you can cook skewers over a campfire.
- **Foil-wrapping.** Some foods can be wrapped in foil and tossed directly into the fire.

Most of the recipes in the barbecue section can just as easily be cooked on a campfire grill. Campfire grilling is similar to barbecuing, in that hot coals are used to cook the food. The difference is the hot coals used with campfire cooking come from wood burnt in the campfire.

There are a number of campfire grills sold in stores and online. You can get a good adjustable grill that allows you to adjust how close the grill is to the coals for less than a hundred bucks. There are fancy campfire grills that come with fire rings to build the fire in, but they tend to be a bit unwieldy and are better suited to backyards where they can be set up and left in place.

Your best bet for campfire cooking is a grill that can be placed over a fire that's already been built. You're still going to have some choices to make. There are swing-away grills that are mounted on a pivot, so you can swing the grill away from the fire for easy access to the food, and there are grills with legs that are set over the top of the campfire, which are generally fixed in place. There are also grills that hang down from a chain, but I've found they tend to be a bit unstable, especially if you've got a lot of food on them or you're trying to balance a pot or pan on one.

Choosing Firewood

Foods grilled over firewood embers are imparted with a smoky flavor that's largely dependent on the type of wood you're burning in the fire. Don't be afraid to experiment until you find a type of wood you like.

Fruit and nut woods are popular, as are oak and hickory. Most people steer clear of pine because it can leave food with an acrid taste and smell. I've used it a couple times and I have to admit it didn't bother me much, but for some the bitter taste is too much.

The following woods are all commonly used for campfire cooking:

- Alder.
- Almond.
- Apple wood.
- Apricot.
- Bay.
- Beech.
- Birch.
- Citrus wood.
- Fruit wood.
- Hickory (only use a little because it imparts a strong taste).
- Maple.
- Mesquite (only use a little because it imparts a strong taste).

- Nut woods.
- Oak.

No matter what type of wood you use, make sure it's dry. Green wood doesn't burn as hot and produces a lot more smoke. You want a clean fire that burns hot, not one that smokes a lot and has trouble staying lit. Use dry wood and you'll have a much better experience.

Making A Campfire

When it comes to campfire grilling, there's one absolute. Without a good fire that burns down to hot embers, you aren't going to be able to properly grill your food. The good news is making a decent campfire is relatively easy.

The following tips should help you get your campfire started in no time at all:

- **Pick a safe place to build your campfire.** If there's a fire pit or fire ring in your campsite, use it. If not, build one and clear the surrounding area of flammable items. Make sure you know local regulations, as there are some areas where campfires are strictly forbidden. Other areas require fires be built only in designated areas or in fire rings.
- **Gather tinder you can use to start your fire.** Tinder is highly flammable material that ignites quickly like crumpled newspaper, dried leaves and dried moss. Dryer lint is great tinder, so if you have a dryer at home, tuck the lint away somewhere for safekeeping until your next camping trip. Place the tinder in the middle of your fire and light the tinder first. It will blaze up quickly, lighting the kindling aflame.
- **The kindling comes next.** Kindling is a step up in size from tinder, but is still highly flammable. Small, dry branches and twigs are usually used as kindling. Wood chips can also be

used. You're going to need a good bit of kindling to get your fire started.

- **Prop the actual firewood up around the tinder and kindling.** Be sure to leave plenty of air room, as stacking too much firewood on a fire you're trying to start will smother it before it can get going. One way to do this is to build a teepee of wood logs around the kindling.
- **Don't be afraid to add more kindling.** If the kindling you've added doesn't look like it's going to get the job done, toss some more kindling onto the fire to keep it going until the firewood gets burning.

For campfire grilling, you're usually going to want to let the fire burn down a bit, so all that remains are hot embers. Small flames are desirable from time to time, but it's usually the hot coals that do the best cooking. Start preparing for dinner early if you plan on campfire cooking because it can take an hour or two to properly prepare the campfire. If you're cooking a meal and you find the embers seem to be dying out, try stirring the embers with a poker to get more oxygen to them. This can really heat things up without have to add more wood and wait for the flames to subside.

Campfire Cooking Recipes

This chapter is packed full of campfire cooking recipes. Each recipe will indicate the method you need to cook it. In order to take full advantage of the campfire cooking recipes, you're going to need the following items:

- A campfire grill.
- Long metal skewers with wood handles.
- Cast iron skillet.
- Cast iron saucepan.

That's it. There's also one recipe that calls for a rotisserie, but you can get by without one.. Easy, huh?

Apple Cider Barbecue Pork Chops

Serving size:

8 servings

Cooking method:

Direct grilling.

Ingredients:

2 to 3 pounds of bone-in pork chops

5 cups apple cider, unsweetened

3 cups water

¾ cup brown sugar

¾ cup sea salt

4 tablespoons onion powder

1 teaspoon ground cinnamon

Salt and pepper, to taste

2 tablespoons extra virgin olive oil

Directions:

1. Combine cider, water, brown sugar, sea salt, onion powder and ground cinnamon in saucepan over low heat. This can be done using a cast iron saucepan placed directly on the grill.
2. Stir until the brown sugar has melted and everything is thoroughly mixed together.
3. Let the brine cool and dump it into a freezer bag.
4. Place pork chops in the freezer bag and let them soak overnight.
5. When you want to cook the pork chops, remove them from the bag and pat them dry.
6. Brush grill with olive oil.
7. Place pork chops on campfire grill directly over the coals.
8. Cook for 10 to 15 minutes, flipping the pork chops halfway through. They're done when they're cooked all the way through.
9. Let the chops sit for 5 to 10 minutes and then serve.

Bacon-Wrapped Drumsticks

Serving size:

8 servings

Cooking method:

Indirect and direct grilling.

Ingredients:

2 pounds chicken drumsticks

1 package thick-sliced bacon

3 tablespoons extra virgin olive oil

1 tablespoon garlic powder

1 tablespoon onion powder

Salt and pepper, to taste

Directions:
1. Cover chicken lightly with olive oil.
2. Combine onion powder and garlic powder and coat chicken.
3. Salt and pepper chicken, to taste.
4. Wrap each of the drumsticks with a slice of bacon.
5. Prepare grill for indirect grilling.
6. Coat grill with light coating of olive oil.
7. Place drumsticks on grill so they aren't directly over the hot embers. The temperature should be between 375 and 400 degrees F.
8. Cook for 15 minutes over indirect heat.
9. Move to direct heat and cook until chicken is done and bacon is crispy. This will usually take an additional 10 to 15 minutes.
10. Remove from grill and cover with foil.
11. Let sit for 10 minutes before serving.

Brown Bag Breakfast Bacon And Eggs

NOTE: This method of cooking takes longer and is messier than simply cooking the bacon and eggs in a skillet. It's also more fun and is an interesting way to cook a meal, so I decided to include it. I learned this method on a Boy Scout campout way back when I was a kid. I hope your kids enjoy it as much as I did.

Serving size:

1 serving

Cooking method:

Paper bag and skewer

Ingredients:

1 brown paper lunch bag

2 eggs

1 slice of bacon

Salt and pepper, to taste

Directions:
1. Break bacon in half and place it inside the bag.
2. Fold the top of the bag down a couple times and pierce it with a skewer or stick.
3. Hold the skewered bag over the coals of the fire. This method won't work if there are open flames because the bag will catch on fire.
4. Let the bacon cook for 5 to 7 minutes.
5. Remove bag from heat and let cool for a couple minutes.
6. Open the bag. Be careful to keep your face away from the bag because hot steam can be released.
7. Add the 2 eggs to the bag and stir them with a fork.
8. Fold the bag and skewer it.
9. Hold the bag over the campfire for an additional 10 to 15 minutes, or until eggs are cooked.
10. Let cool for 5 minutes and eat while still warm.

Beef Skewers

Serving size:

8 servings

Cooking method:

Skewer

Ingredients:

3 pounds beef, cut into 1" cubes

Red and green peppers, cut into 1" cubes

Whole cherry tomatoes

Whole mushrooms

¼ cup extra virgin olive oil

Salt and pepper, to taste

Directions:
1. Place meat and veggies on skewer, alternating items.
2. Brush olive oil over the steak.
3. Cook over an open flame until the steak is cooked to your liking. Coat with olive oil any time you notice the steak starting to look dry. This will take 10 to 20 minutes, depending on how well you want the steak to be done.
4. Season with salt and pepper, to taste.
5. Let cool for 5 minutes.
6. Pull off skewers and eat.

Bannock Bread

Serving size:

8 to 12 servings

Cooking method:

Skewer

Ingredients:

4 cups flour

1 cup water

2 ½ tablespoons baking powder

3 tablespoons butter, melted

Directions:

1. Add all ingredients except water to a bowl and stir together.
2. Add water a few tablespoons at a time and knead in until the dough becomes a thick consistency. Be careful not to add too much water. The dough should be thick, but pliable.
3. Remove a chunk of dough and wrap it around the end of a skewer. Form it around the skewer so it won't fall off.
4. Hold it over the hot embers of the fire until the dough is cooked and the outside has browned. This takes anywhere from 8 to 12 minutes. Rotate skewer regularly to ensure the bread cooks evenly.
5. Eat as-is or drizzle with honey before eating.

Blueberry Pancakes

Serving size:

6 to 8 servings

Cooking method:

Skillet on campfire grill

Ingredients:

2 cups flour

2 large eggs

2 cups fresh blueberries

1 ½ cups milk

1 cup sour cream

1 stick unsalted butter, melted

1 teaspoon vanilla extract

1 teaspoon baking powder

3 tablespoons sugar

½ teaspoon salt

Directions:

1. Combine all of the ingredients except the blueberries and whisk together in a bowl.
2. Add the blueberries and fold them into the batter.
3. Place the skillet over the campfire and let it heat up.
4. Oil the skillet and pout ¼ to ½ cup of batter into the skillet.
5. Cook the pancakes on one side until bubbles start to form on the surface and then flip them over and cook the other side.
6. The pancakes are done when they're golden brown on each side. Serve with syrup or your favorite topping.

Campfire Quesadilla

Serving size:

1 serving

Cooking method:

Foil-wrapped and direct grilled

Ingredients:

1 flour tortilla

½ cup Mexican blend cheese

Any meats or veggies you'd like to add

Directions:
1. Place tortilla on a piece of foil.
2. Add cheese and other ingredients to the tortilla. Beef, chicken and shrimp are good meats to add. You can also add bell peppers, onions and mushrooms for a loaded quesadilla. Cook the meat and veggies in a skillet before placing them in the tortilla.
3. Fold both ends of the tortilla over one another.
4. Fold the aluminum foil over the top of the quesadilla.
5. Place the foil packet over direct heat and cook until the cheese is melted.

Dad's Quick And Easy Tri Tip

Serving size:

6 to 8 servings

Cooking method:

Direct and indirect grilling

Ingredients:

1 tri tip

4 cloves garlic, minced

1 teaspoon black pepper

1 teaspoon fresh lime juice

1 cup olive oil

3 tablespoons Pappy's seasoning

Directions:
1. Combine all marinade ingredients in a large freezer bag and shake until blended.
2. Place tri tip in bag and let marinate overnight.
3. Prepare grill for direct grilling.
4. Place tri tip on grill over the coals and cook for 6 to 8 minutes on each side.
5. Move tri tip to an area further away from the coals to complete grilling. Cook tri tip for an addition 5 to 10 minutes on each side, depending on how done you want it to be.
6. Let the tri tip sit for 8 to 10 minutes before slicing and serving it.

Easy Beer-Battered Fish Fillets

Serving size:

8 servings.

Cooking method:

Cast iron skillet placed on grill over campfire.

Ingredients:

8 fish fillets

8 lemon halves

2 cups buttermilk pancake mix

2 cups beer

½ cup extra virgin olive oil

Salt and vinegar, to taste

Directions:

1. Combine buttermilk pancake mix with beer and stir until mixed.
2. Place olive oil in cast iron skillet and place on grill over campfire. You want to have the grill at the lowest possible setting. Let the olive oil heat up for 5 minutes.
3. Dip the fish fillets in the batter and drop them in the skillet. The oil has to be hot enough to fry the fish fillet or the fillets won't properly cook.
4. Cook the fillets until golden brown on both sides.
5. Squeeze lemon over filets and garnish with salt and vinegar, to taste.

Easy Omelets

NOTE: These omelets can just as easily be cooked on a Dutch oven lid flipped upside down and placed in the coals of the campfire.

Serving size:

1 to 2 servings

Cooking method:

Skillet on campfire grill

Ingredients:

3 eggs

3 strips bacon, cooked and crumbled.

3 sausage links, cooked and crumbled

10 sliced mushrooms

Spinach, to your liking

½ cup cheddar cheese

Directions:

1. Add the 3 eggs to the skillet and stir them with a spatula.
2. Add the spinach and mushrooms and stir them into the eggs.
3. Spread the eggs out across the pan.
4. Let them cook for a few minutes and then add the bacon and sausage to the middle of the omelet.
5. Fold the eggs over the top of the bacon and sausage.
6. Sprinkle cheese on top and serve warm.

Foil-Wrapped Baked Potatoes

Serving size:

1 potato

Cooking method:

Foil-wrapping

Ingredients:

1 potato

1 tablespoon butter

Toppings (sour cream, chives, cheese, bacon bits, etc.)

Directions:

1. Cut a slit in the top of the potato and spread butter across the top.
2. Wrap potato in aluminum foil. Double-wrapping works best because it protects the potato from scorching.
3. Bury the potato in the coals of the fire.
4. Let it sit for 45 minute to an hour, or until the potato is soft like a normal baked potato.
5. Let cool for 5 to 10 minutes and unwrap.
6. Top with your favorite toppings and enjoy.

Foil-Wrapped Cheesy Potatoes

Serving size:

1 serving

Cooking method:

Foil-wrapping

Ingredients:

1 large potato

½ medium onion, chopped

½ clove garlic, minced

3 tablespoons crumbled bacon

¼ cup cheddar cheese

¼ cup mozzarella cheese

1 tablespoon butter

½ teaspoon sea salt

½ teaspoon pepper

Directions:

1. Cut the potato into cubes.
2. Add all of the ingredients to a foil wrap and wrap it up tightly.
3. Place the foil wrap into the hot embers of your campfire for 15 to 20 minutes, or until potatoes are cooked and cheese is melted.
4. Let cool for 10 minutes and eat.

Foil-Wrapped Ground Beef Veggie Stew

Serving size:

1 serving per foil wrap

Cooking method:

Skillet and foil-wrapping

Ingredients:

½ pound hamburger

½ cup water

1 carrot, cut into coins

½ medium onion, diced

1 stick celery, chopped into small pieces

½ clove garlic, minced

1 tablespoon basil, chopped

1 can cream of mushroom soup

Directions:

1. Brown hamburger in a skillet.
2. Make a cup out of aluminum foil.
3. Add all ingredients to the cup and stir up.
4. Fold aluminum foil over the top of the cup and place the cup directly in the hot embers of the fire.
5. Let cook for 15 minutes, or until veggies are cooked to your liking.
6. Let cool for 10 minutes and serve warm.

Foil-Wrapped Lemon Garlic Fish

Serving size:

1 serving

Cooking method:

Foil-wrapping

Ingredients:

1 fish filet

¼ cup water

Half a lemon

10 cherry tomatoes, halved

1 small garlic clove, minced

½ teaspoon lemon salt

Cracked black pepper, to taste

Directions:
1. Place fish in foil.
2. Squeeze the lemon over the fish.
3. Place cherry tomato halves around the fish.
4. Season with garlic, lemon salt and cracked black pepper.
5. Add water and close foil wrap.
6. Place foil wrap directly into hot embers of campfire.
7. Let cook for 15 to 20 minutes, or until fish is cooked all the way through and flaky.

Foil-Wrapped Popcorn

Serving size:
2 to 4 servings

Cooking method:
Foil-wrapping

Ingredients:

¼ cup popcorn

5 tablespoons vegetable oil

Salt and melted butter, to taste

Directions:

1. Place unpopped popcorn in the center of a large piece of foil.
2. Drizzle the oil over the popcorn.
3. Fold the edges of the foil up to the center. You're going to want to leave plenty of room for the popcorn to pop.
4. Make sure the edges are sealed and place the foil packet in the hot embers of the fire.
5. Let sit until the popcorn stops popping. It helps if you shake the packet from time to time.
6. Remove from fire and carefully open the packet. There will be a lot of hot steam inside, so be extremely careful.
7. Add butter and salt to your liking and enjoy.

Foil-Wrapped Rainbow Trout

Serving size:

1 serving

Cooking method:

Foil-wrapping

Ingredients:

1 pan size rainbow trout

1 whole lemon

1 tablespoon butter

Salt and pepper, to taste

Directions:

1. Clean trout and remove fins, head and tail.
2. Slice lemon into wedges.
3. Squeeze lemon juice over trout.
4. Add lemon wedges, trout, butter and salt and pepper to a foil packet and wrap it up tightly.
5. Place foil wrap directly in the campfire and cook for 5 to 10 minutes on each side, or until fish is flaky when you touch it with a fork.
6. Let cool until warm and enjoy.

Foil-Wrapped Zucchini

Serving size:

1 serving

Cooking method:

Foil-wrapping.

Ingredients:

1 whole zucchini, sliced into wedges

Extra-virgin olive oil

Salt and pepper, to taste

Directions:

1. Cut zucchini into wedges.
2. Place on foil.
3. Drizzle with olive oil.
4. Season with salt and pepper, to taste.
5. Fold foil over the top and fold up edges, so juice doesn't spill out while the zucchini is cooking.
6. Place foil-wrapped zucchini directly in hot embers of fire.
7. Cook for 10 to 15 minutes, or until zucchini is cooked to your liking.
8. Let cool for 5 to 10 minutes and serve warm.

Garlic Thyme Game Hens

Serving size:

1 game hen per serving

Cooking method:

Direct grilling.

Ingredients:

1 Cornish game hen

A bunch of fresh thyme

1 clove of garlic, minced

1 tablespoon freshly ground black pepper

1 teaspoon coarse salt

1 tablespoon extra-virgin olive oil

Directions:

1. Make sure game hens are thawed before being placed on the grill.
2. Coat the game hen with olive oil.
3. Chop thyme and garlic into fine pieces and rub it all over the game hen.
4. Rub salt and pepper into game hen.
5. Let the game hen marinate for at least a couple hours.
6. Place grill over campfire for direct grilling.
7. Place game hens on grill and cook for 12 to 15 minutes on each side. Cook time depends on how hot the fire is and the size of the game hen.
8. When done the game hen will be crispy brown and will have grill marks on both sides. To add an interesting flavor to the game hens, toss some of the thyme onto the fire and let the smoke infuse into the meat.
9. Remove from grill and let sit for 10 minutes before serving.

Grilled Oysters

Serving size:

6 to 8 servings

Cooking method:

Direct grilling.

Ingredients:

30 oysters

Tabasco sauce or lemon juice for seasoning (optional)

Directions:

1. Place the oysters on the grill over direct heat.
2. They're ready to eat when they pop open.
3. Season with tabasco sauce or lemon juice, or just eat them the way they are.

Grilled Turkey Drumsticks

Serving size:

6 servings

Cooking method:

Indirect and direct grilling.

Ingredients:

6 turkey drumsticks

4 tablespoons garlic powder

4 tablespoons cumin

4 tablespoons sea salt

1 tablespoon cayenne pepper

1 tablespoon black pepper

6 tablespoons extra virgin olive oil

Directions:

1. Prepare campfire for indirect cooking by creating an area beneath the grill where there are no embers.
2. Mix all of the dry seasonings together in a bowl.
3. Rub turkey drumsticks with olive oil.
4. Rub seasonings into drumsticks.
5. Sear the drumsticks over direct heat for 4 to 5 minutes on each side in order to lock moisture and flavor in.
6. Move to indirect heat and cook for 60 to 90 minutes, or until internal temperature of drumsticks reach at least 180 degrees F. Brush with olive oil a couple times while cooking.
7. Remove from grill and let sit for 10 minutes before serving.

Simple Grilled Rib Eye

Serving size:

4 servings

Cooking method:

Direct grilling

Ingredients:

2 ½ pounds rib eye steak

2 tablespoons fresh cracked black pepper

2 tablespoons sea salt

3 tablespoons extra virgin olive oil

Directions:
1. Bring steaks to room temperature before grilling them.
2. Brush steaks with olive oil.
3. Rub sea salt and cracked black pepper into the steaks.
4. Rub olive oil on grill.
5. Place steaks on grill over direct heat.
6. Cook for 6 to 10 minutes on each side, or until steak is done to your liking.
7. Let steaks sit for 10 minutes.
8. Serve with steak sauce or enjoy as-is.

Skewer Croissant Dogs

Serving size:

8 servings

Cooking method:

Skewer

Ingredients:

8 hot dogs

2 packs of ready to bake croissants

Directions:

1. Place hot dogs on skewers.
2. Open croissant package and wrap around hot dogs.
3. Cook over direct heat by using the skewers to hold the croissant dogs over the fire.
4. Cook until hot dogs are cooked and the croissants are lightly browned.

Stuffed Jalapenos

Serving size:

16 servings

Cooking method:

Direct grilling

Ingredients:

8 large jalapenos

4 slices bacon, cooked until crispy

½ cup shredded Mexican blend cheese

½ of a medium onion, chopped into fine pieces

1 garlic clove, minced

1 tablespoon lime juice

½ teaspoon sea salt

Cilantro, for garnishing

Directions:

1. Prepare grill for direct grilling.
2. Cook bacon in skillet until crispy.
3. Crumble bacon.
4. Combine all stuffing ingredients in a bowl and stir together.
5. Cut jalapenos in half and remove seeds.
6. Fill jalapeno halves with stuffing.
7. Cook on grill for 10 minutes, or until cheese on top started to brown and the jalapeno is cooked all the way through.
8. Garnish with cilantro and serve warm.

Roasted Potatoes

Serving size:

8 servings

Cooking method:

Pot and skillet over direct heat

Ingredients:

4 pounds new potatoes

¼ cup extra virgin olive oil

3 tablespoon thyme

3 tablespoon oregano

3 tablespoons paprika

2 tablespoons garlic salt

2 teaspoons black pepper

Directions:

1. Boil the potatoes for 10 minutes in a pot.
2. Cut the potatoes into wedges and coat them with olive oil.
3. Sprinkle seasoning on potatoes.
4. Cook potatoes in a skillet over direct heat until they're browned on all sides.

Rotisserie Leg Of Lamb

NOTE: If you don't have a rotisserie, you can cook the leg of lamb over indirect heat. Be sure to turn it regularly and watch it closely.

Serving size:

10 to 15 servings

Cooking method:

Rotisserie

Ingredients:

1 5-pound leg of lamb roast

2 cups white wine

1 cup extra virgin olive oil

Fresh thyme

Fresh oregano

Fresh savory

2 cloves of garlic

Salt and cracked black pepper, to taste

Directions:

1. Use a knife to poke holes in the leg of lamb.
2. Combine pepper, thyme, oregano, savory and garlic and chop the herbs up finely.
3. Push the herb and pepper mixture into each of the holes. Alternatively, you can push entire sprigs of the herbs into the holes.
4. Brush the leg of lamb with olive oil.
5. Rub spices, garlic and salt into the exterior.
6. Place the white wine in a sealable plastic bag and place the roast in the bag. Seal the bag and let it marinate for 6 hours. Keep on ice or refrigerated while marinating.

7. Prepare the fire for rotisserie roasting. You want there to be a good amount of heat coming off the fire.
8. Insert the rotisserie shaft into the rack of lamb and spear it lengthwise.
9. Rub salt and pepper into the rack of lamb and place it on the rotisserie over the fire.
10. Slowly turn the rotisserie. This is where an electric rotisserie really comes in handy because it does the hard part for you.
11. Brush every 15 minutes with olive oil mixed with herbs.
12. The leg of lamb will take 50 minutes to 65 minutes to cook, if you've got the heat right. It will turn golden brown and the inside will be medium rare.
13. Remove the leg of lamb from the rotisserie and wrap it in foil. Let it sit for 30 minutes before cutting and serving.

Sausage And Cheese Skewers

Serving size:

1 serving

Cooking method:

Skewer

Ingredients:

1 sausage

1 slice of your favorite cheese

Hot dog bun

Directions:

1.	Place sausage on skewer and cook until it starts to brown and drip juices.
2.	Drape a slice of cheese over the sausage and carefully extend the skewer over the campfire to melt the cheese and brown it slightly. This requires a fair bit of balance, so children should be helped by an adult.
3.	Place sausage and cheese in a hot dog bun.
4.	Let cool for 5 to 10 minutes and eat when warm.

Tandoori Chicken

NOTE: This chicken is spicy and isn't for the faint of heart. I love it, but if you don't like your food with a bit of a kick, you probably won't appreciate tandoori chicken.

Serving size:

8 servings

Cooking method:

Direct grilling

Ingredients:

8 chicken breasts

1 onion, finely chopped

1 jalapeno pepper, deseeded and chopped

1 clove garlic, minced

4 tablespoons fresh ginger, finely chopped

1 lemon

1 cup plain yogurt

3 tablespoons tandoori masala

3 tablespoons sea salt

3 teaspoons ground cumin

3 teaspoons turmeric

4 tablespoons olive oil

Directions:
1. Poke a bunch of holes in the chicken breasts.
2. Add all of the ingredients except the chicken to a blender and blend until smooth.
3. Place chicken and marinade in a freezer bag. Be sure to coat all of the pieces of chicken with the marinade.
4. Refrigerate or keep in ice chest on ice overnight.
5. Prepare grill for direct grilling.

6. Cook the chicken breasts for 10 minutes on each side, or until cooked to your liking.
7. Remove from grill and let sit for 5 to 10 minutes before serving.

Veggie Foil Wraps

Serving size:

1 serving

Cooking method:

Foil-wrapping

Ingredients:

Half a lemon, cut into wedges

1 small carrot, cut into coins

1 small potato, cut into wedges

3 to 5 small cherry tomatoes

3 to 5 small mushrooms

¼ bell pepper, sliced into pieces

¼ medium onion, sliced

½ cup water

1 clove garlic, minced

1 tablespoon extra-virgin olive oil

Salt and pepper, to taste

A dash of cayenne pepper

Large piece of aluminum foil

Directions:
1. Make a large cup out of the aluminum foil.
2. Line the bottom of the cup with lemon wedges.
3. Add the vegetables and water to the cup.
4. Add the olive oil, salt and cayenne pepper.
5. Fold the top of the cup closed and place it directly in the hot embers of your campfire.
6. Cook for 20 to 30 minutes, or until vegetables are cooked to your liking.
7. Let cool for 10 minutes and enjoy!

The Dutch Oven

Most campers have never heard of a Dutch oven, let alone actually used one to cook a meal. I was guilty as charged until a friend of ours brought one along on camping trip a few years back and opened up a whole new world of campfire cooking for our family.

A Dutch oven is a flat-bottomed kettle made of cast metal that allows you to cook a wide variety of soups, stews, meats and tasty desserts and pastries in an oven-like setting. You place your food inside the oven and then place a heavy cast iron lid on it. The oven is then placed directly in the hot coals of the campfire and coals are added to the top of the lid. The inside of the Dutch oven gets very hot, cooking your food in a manner similar to if you were using your oven at home.

You can find a number of sizes of Dutch ovens, ranging from small to huge. You may be tempted to go with one of the smaller Dutch ovens like the 8" or 10" sizes because they'll be easy to lug around. I've found these to be a bit lacking when it comes to campfire cooking, especially when you're bringing larger groups camping. You can underfill a larger 12" to 14" oven when there are less people. You can't overfill an oven that's too small. You aren't going to want to cook up multiple batches, so get a bigger oven and you'll be able to handle all but the biggest of camping groups.

A Dutch oven can be used to stew, bake and roast a wide variety of foods. You can also flip the lid over and use the curved surface to fry stuff like eggs and potatoes. If you haven't used a Dutch oven before, you're going to be surprised at how versatile a cooking tool it is. Once you start using one, you'll wonder how you lived without it.

The best part about using a Dutch oven to cook is they're a fun and easy way to cook a meal big enough for the entire family. You prepare the food and place the oven in the campfire, and the fire does the work for you. The most you'll usually have to do after that is stir the contents of the pot a couple times as it cooks.

Cast Iron vs. Aluminum

There's much debate between Dutch oven aficionados as to whether cast iron or aluminum is the best material for a Dutch oven to be made from. Cast iron is the traditionalist's choice because it's been in use since before the pioneers came to America. Aluminum is a fairly new player in the game and aluminum Dutch ovens have only been around for a short period of time.

I've tried both and have found them to be equally effective at cooking food, with a few quirks specific to each type of metal. I haven't found one to be particularly better than the other, especially when it comes to the higher quality Dutch ovens on the market.

Cast iron is heavier than aluminum, which can be a bit of a double-edged sword. It's stronger and more durable, but is heavier and harder to carry around. If weight is of concern, you're probably better off going with an aluminum model. For most campers, this isn't going to be an issue because you're only going to be packing it from your car to a nearby campsite.

When it comes to cooking food evenly, cast iron is the clear winner. Cast iron heats up slowly and food is cooked evenly. Food will cook faster in an aluminum Dutch oven, but it may cook unevenly as different area of the oven heat up at a different pace.

Aluminum Dutch ovens are easier to clean than cast iron ovens. You can use soap and water on an aluminum oven, while all you're supposed to use on a cast iron oven is water. Cast iron ovens also have to be seasoned with vegetable oil, which is a bit of a hassle, but is fairly easy once you know what you're doing. Aluminum ovens can also be seasoned, but it isn't a requirement like it is with cast iron ovens.

To be completely honest, the differences between the two types of Dutch oven are so minor, you might not notice them at all if I hadn't just pointed them out. It all boils down to whether you want even cooking at expense of a bit of convenience or whether you're willing to sacrifice a little convenience in order to use an oven that's slightly better when it comes to cooking.

Seasoning A Dutch Oven

There are a number of reasons you should season your Dutch oven:

- To prevent rust.
- To prevent corrosion.
- It makes it easier to clean.
- Food tastes better when cooked in a seasoned Dutch oven.
- It creates a non-stick cooking surface.
- It removes contaminants.

While both aluminum and cast iron Dutch ovens can be seasoned, it's more critical that you season cast iron Dutch ovens because they're more prone to pitting and rust if they aren't seasoned. I still recommend seasoning aluminum Dutch ovens because they can also rust; they just aren't as likely to as the cast iron ovens.

The initial seasoning of a Dutch oven is the most important one because it prepares the Dutch oven for cooking and removes the wax-like protectant most factories coat their ovens with before shipping. Before seasoning, give the Dutch oven a good scrubbing with soap and water to remove the wax. Use a scouring pad to ensure you remove all of it. After the initial cleansing, you don't want to use soap and water on cast iron Dutch ovens. It's OK to use soap and water on aluminum Dutch ovens for future cleansings.

Here are the steps required for the first seasoning of a Dutch oven:

1. Seasoning can be done in either a large barbecue or your oven. If you do it in your oven, make sure you place a drip tray beneath the rack the Dutch oven is on to catch any oil that drips off while you're seasoning it. This is a critical step because vegetable oil can be highly flammable.

2.	After washing your Dutch oven, place it on the grill or in the oven for 5 minutes at 350 degrees F to ensure it's been properly dried.
3.	Once it's dry, remove the Dutch oven from the oven and rub vegetable shortening all over the entire surface of the oven. You want to use regular shortening, not butter or some other shortening substitute. Make sure you rub it into every nook, cranny and corner of the oven.
4.	Flip the Dutch oven upside down and place it on the grill or in the oven. This will allow the shortening to run out of the Dutch oven as it melts. You can place the lid on top of the Dutch oven or you can wait and cook it separately.
5.	Cook the Dutch oven for an hour at 350 degrees F. It might get a bit smoky, which is why most people opt to use a large barbecue if they have one. Open a few windows in your house if you're doing it in your oven.
6.	After an hour has passed, let the Dutch oven cool for 30 minutes and then use paper towels to remove any excess oil from the oven.
7.	Repeat steps 3 through 6 at least one more time to ensure proper seasoning.
8.	Let the oven completely cool and remove all excess oil. Congrats! You've got a properly seasoned Dutch oven.

If you cook a lot of fatty foods in your Dutch oven, it will probably never need to be reseasoned again because the fats and oils in your foods will season it as you cook them. If you cook a lot of acidic foods, you may find you need to occasionally season your oven because food is starting to stick to it. If you need to season your Dutch oven again, just follow the steps in the previous tutorial without using soap and water.

Temperature Control

Most Dutch oven recipes call for cooking food at a certain temperature. The most popular method involves counting the number of coals you place both beneath and above the Dutch oven. It's a somewhat decent method of temperature control when you're using charcoal because all of the coals will be equal in size. The coal counting method falls flat on its face when you're cooking using a campfire because you aren't going to get equal sized coals out of your campfire.

Because coal counting charcoal pieces works well, a lot of people opt to use charcoal in their campfires when it comes time to cook with a Dutch oven. If you want to use this method, all you have to do is add a pile of charcoal to the campfire and move it away from the fire once it's lit.

The general rule of thumb is to take the diameter of the Dutch oven and double it and that's the number of pieces of charcoal it will take to get the oven to 350 degrees F. Create a ring of charcoal beneath the oven that's missing every other coal and then put the rest of the coals on top. Each additional coal you add to the top will increase the internal temperature of the oven by approximately 15 to 20 degrees F. Coals placed on top of the Dutch oven should be spread out evenly.

If you have a 14" Dutch oven, you would start with 28 briquettes. Make a ring around the bottom and remove every other coal. Place the coals you removed from the ring and the rest of the coals on top. You'll now have an internal temperature close to 350 degrees F. Now, let's say your recipe calls for cooking at 400 degrees F. Adding 3 coals to the top will get you pretty close to 400 degrees F.

Other campfire cooks opt to place the Dutch oven directly in the coals of the fire. They throw some coals on top and watch the food they're cooking closely. They don't worry about temperature too much, instead opting to keep a close eye on the food they're cooking.

It isn't as accurate as the coal counting method, which truth be told isn't all that accurate itself, but I've used it to successfully cook a number of campfire meals when I don't feel like being bothered lighting charcoal in the campfire and counting the coals I'm using. Cooking using this method requires keeping an eye on your food and adding coals if it looks like it's cooking too slow and removing coals if it's cooking too fast. You're also going to want to rotate your pot and stir your food more frequently because hotspots can develop that'll make certain areas of the pot hotter than others.

If you really want to get technical, you can buy a Dutch oven thermometer that'll tell you the temperature inside the Dutch oven. This will allow you to closely gauge the temperatures at which you're cooking your food.

Dutch Oven Recipes

If you're like I was when I first started cooking with a Dutch oven, you're going to be shocked at the sheer variety of items you can cook in a Dutch oven. I've taken entire camping trips in which I've only used my Dutch oven. I'm also guilty of building a fire pit in my back yard, so I can enjoy Dutch oven recipes at home when I'm not camping.

If you have any Dutch oven recipes you love that you'd like to see in future iterations of this book, drop me a line at the e-mail address at the end of the book. I'm always on the hunt for new recipes to try out and I'd love to hear from you!

Barbecue Beans

Serving size:

8 to 10 servings

Cooking method:

Dutch oven

Cooking Temperature:

350 degrees F

Ingredients:

1 pound bacon, cooked and crumbled

4 16-ounce cans of kidney beans

1 large can pork and beans

1 medium onion, chopped

½ cup ketchup

½ cup barbecue sauce

½ cup brown sugar

3 tablespoons mustard

1 teaspoon salt

1 teaspoon black pepper

Directions:
1. Prepare Dutch oven for cooking at 350 degrees F.
2. Add all sauce ingredients to the oven and stir together.
3. Add the rest of the ingredients and stir.
4. Place lid on Dutch oven and cook for 60 minutes.
5. Remove lid and stir every 15 minutes.
6. Serve warm.

Beef Stew

Serving size:
6 to 8 servings
Cooking method:
Dutch oven

Cooking Temperature:
350 degrees F
Ingredients:
3 pounds steak, cubed
3 cups water
4 carrots
2 potatoes, peeled and cubed
1 onion, chopped
1 cup mushrooms, sliced
Salt and pepper, to taste
Directions:
1. Prepare Dutch oven for cooking at 350 degrees F.
2. Add all of the ingredients to the oven and stir together.
3. Cook for 45 minutes to an hour with the lid on, or until potatoes and carrots are soft.
4. Serve warm.

Blueberry Cinnamon Rolls

NOTE: This recipe is a bit more difficult than most of the other recipes in the book, but it's pretty easy once you get the hang of it. You can make the filling at home and bring it along to speed things up a bit.

Serving size:

6 servings

Cooking method:

Dutch oven

Cooking Temperature:

375 degrees F

Cinnamon Roll Ingredients:

3 cups flour

1 cup milk

¼ cup vegetable oil

¼ cup sugar

1 ½ teaspoons active dry yeast

½ teaspoon baking powder

½ teaspoon baking soda

½ teaspoon salt

Filling Ingredients:

2 cups blueberries

½ cup water

4 tablespoons sugar

2 tablespoons cinnamon

1 tablespoon honey

3 teaspoons lemon juice

2 teaspoons corn starch

Cream cheese frosting, for topping

Directions:
1. Make the filling first.
2. Combine all of the filling ingredients in a Dutch oven placed into a campfire.
3. Stir until the mixture thickens.
4. Remove from heat and let cool.
5. Remove the filling from the Dutch oven, so you can use it to bake the cinnamon rolls.
6. Add milk and sugar to a saucepan and bring it to a simmer.
7. Remove it from the saucepan and let it cool until it's lukewarm.
8. Add the yeast to the milk and stir it in.
9. Add the flour and stir it in.
10. Add the rest of the ingredients and stir them in.
11. Let dough rise for an hour and then punch it down.
12. Roll the dough out on a flat surface.
13. Cut the dough into long rectangle shapes.
14. Spread the filling across the top of the dough.
15. Roll the dough so that the filling is on the inside of the cinnamon roll.
16. Grease the Dutch oven and place each cinnamon roll in it when you're done rolling it.
17. Let rolls sit in the Dutch oven for an additional 45 minutes.
18. Place the Dutch oven in the hot embers of the fire and place coals on top.
19. Cook for 15 to 20 minutes, or until cinnamon rolls are golden brown.
20. Remove Dutch oven from fire and remove lid.
21. Smear cream cheese frosting over the top of the cinnamon rolls.
22. Serve warm.

Cinnamon Apple Crisp

Serving size:

8 to 10 servings

Cooking method:

Dutch oven

Cooking Temperature:

350 degrees F

Ingredients:

10 apples, peeled and sliced

2 cups brown sugar

3 teaspoons cinnamon

1 ½ cups flour

1 stick of butter

2 ½ cups oats

2 teaspoons nutmeg

1 teaspoon baking powder

1 teaspoon vanilla extract

Directions:
1. Combine cinnamon, sugar and nutmeg in a bowl.
2. Place apple slices in bowl and coat with cinnamon sugar.
3. Add the rest of the ingredients and the remaining cinnamon sugar to a bowl and mix together until thoroughly mixed.
4. Divide the mixture in half and press half into the bottom of the Dutch oven.
5. Add the apples on top of this layer.
6. Place the rest of the crust mixture onto the top of the apples.
7. Bake at 375 degrees F for 30 to 45 minutes, or until the apples are cooked tender.
8. Let cool and serve lukewarm.

Cheesy Bacon Rolls

Serving size:

6 to 8 servings

Cooking method:

Dutch oven

Cooking Temperature:

350 degrees F

Ingredients:

Dinner rolls

1 cup crumbled bacon

½ cup butter

2 cups grated cheddar cheese

1 cup grated mozzarella cheese

Directions:

1. Prepare Dutch oven for cooking at 350 degrees F.
2. Melt butter and coat dinner rolls with melted butter.
3. Place in Dutch oven and cover with cheese.
4. Sprinkle crumbled bacon generously across the top.
5. Place lid on Dutch oven and bake for a half hour, or until cheese melts and starts to brown.
6. Serve warm.

Chicken Fajitas

Serving size:

8 to 12 servings

Cooking method:

Dutch oven

Cooking Temperature:

350 degrees F

Ingredients:

2 pounds chicken breasts, cut into strips

1 onion, sliced

1 red bell pepper, sliced

1 green bell pepper, sliced

1 4-ounce can of green chilies

3 tablespoons olive oil

2 tablespoons chili powder

2 teaspoons cumin

1 teaspoon garlic powder

½ teaspoon cayenne pepper (optional)

½ teaspoon salt

Flour tortillas

Directions:

1. Add chicken and veggies to the Dutch oven.
2. Drizzle olive oil over the chicken and veggies.
3. Combine spices in a small bowl.
4. Add spices to chicken and vegetables and stir until coated.
5. Place Dutch oven in campfire.
6. Place lid on Dutch oven and place coals on lid.
7. Cook for 20 to 30 minutes, or until chicken is cooked all the way through.

Chili Con Carne

Serving size:

10 servings

Cooking method:

Dutch oven

Cooking Temperature:

375 degrees F

Ingredients:

4 pounds ground beef

2 medium onions, chopped

3 cans of diced tomatoes

3 cans kidney beans

¼ cup water

2 tablespoons extra virgin olive oil

3 teaspoons oregano

2 teaspoons salt

2 teaspoons Worcestershire sauce

2 teaspoons ground cumin

1 teaspoon chili powder

½ teaspoon cayenne pepper (add more for hotter chili)

Shredded cheddar cheese, for topping

Directions:
1. Heat Dutch oven to 375 degrees F.
2. Add olive oil to oven.
3. Brown hamburger in the oven.
4. Chop the onions and add them to the oven.
5. Cook the onions until they start to turn clear.

6. Add the rest of the ingredients except for the beans and stir together.
7. Place lid on Dutch oven and place coals on top of lid.
8. Cook chili for 45 minutes.
9. Remove the lid and add the beans.
10. Let the chili cook for another 45 minutes with the lid off.
11. Top with shredded cheddar and serve warm.

Caramel Apple Pie

Serving size:

5 to 7 servings

Cooking method:

Dutch oven

Cooking Temperature:

375 degrees F

Ingredients:

8 to 10 baking apples, sliced thinly and peeled

3 tablespoons fresh lime juice

1 cup granulated sugar

1 whole egg

½ cup flour

½ cup sour cream

2 tablespoons butter

2 teaspoons cinnamon

1 ½ teaspoons nutmeg

1 teaspoon vanilla

½ teaspoon salt

Pastry dough, for crust

Topping Ingredients:

1 cup caramel

1 cup chopped pecans

Directions:
1. Line the Dutch oven with foil.
2. Coat apple slices with lime juice.
3. Combine all of the ingredients and stir together until thoroughly mixed.
4. Lay pastry crust down to form bottom crust.

5. Spread apple filling out across the bottom crust.
6. Place another crust over the top.
7. Cut a few vent slits into the dough on top.
8. Prepare Dutch oven for cooking at 375 degrees F.
9. Cook for 50 to 60 minutes, or until the crust is golden brown.
10. Remove Dutch oven from fire and let pie cool to lukewarm before serving.
11. Mix caramel and pecans together.
12. Drizzle over the top of the pie before serving.
   0.

Cola Chicken

Serving size:

8 servings

Cooking method:

Dutch oven

Cooking Temperature:

350 degrees F

Ingredients:

8 pieces of chicken

1 can of cola

½ cup ketchup

½ cup barbecue sauce

Directions:

1. Prepare Dutch oven for cooking at 350 degrees F.
2. Add ketchup, cola and barbecue sauce to Dutch oven.
3. Add chicken and spoon sauce over the top of the chicken.
4. Place lid on Dutch oven and cook for 30 minutes.
5. Lift lid and spoon more sauce over the chicken.
6. Cook for another 45 minutes to an hour, or until chicken is cooked all the way through.

Cornbread

Serving size:

6 to 8 servings

Cooking method:

Dutch oven

Cooking Temperature:

350 degrees F

Ingredients:

5 eggs

2 cups milk

2 cups cornmeal

2 ½ cups flour

1 cup butter

1 cup sugar

1 ½ tablespoons baking powder

1 teaspoon salt

Directions:

1. Add dry ingredients to a bowl and stir together.
2. Combine wet ingredients and blend together.
3. Add dry ingredients to wet ingredients and stir them in slowly.
4. Prepare Dutch oven for cooking at 350 degrees F.
5. Grease the inside of the oven.
6. Pour corn bread batter into the oven.
7. Cook with lid on for an hour to an hour and a half, or until cornbread is cooked all the way through and golden brown on top.
8. Serve warm with butter or honey.

Corn Chowder

Serving size:

8 to 12 servings

Cooking method:

Dutch oven

Cooking Temperature:

350 degrees F

Ingredients:

6 cups frozen corn kernels, defrosted

4 cups water

1 cup of heavy cream

5 slices of bacon, crumbled

1 medium onion, chopped

1 pound small red potatoes, cut into chunks

¼ cup flour

¼ stick butter

2 teaspoons thyme

2 teaspoons basil

1 ½ teaspoons salt

2 teaspoons black pepper

Directions:

1. Prepare Dutch oven for cooking at 350 degrees F.
2. Melt butter in Dutch oven.
3. Add onion, bacon, thyme, basil, salt and pepper.
4. Cook until onions turn clear and start to soften. Stir often.
5. Add flour and stir in quickly.
6. Add water and bring to a rolling boil.
7. Add the corn and potatoes and stir into the chowder.

8. Let simmer until the potatoes are cooked. This usually takes anywhere from 20 to 30 minutes.
9. Add heavy cream and stir in.
10. Let it simmer for another 10 minutes.
11. Season with salt and pepper to your liking and serve warm.

Easy "Sourdough" Bread

NOTE: To all the sourdough purists—Yes, I'm aware this technically isn't real sourdough bread, but I don't have the patience or wherewithal to cook the real thing. This recipe is much easier and it tastes pretty dang good, at least to my unrefined palate. And it can be whipped up in a few hours instead of taking days, like most real sourdough recipes.

Serving size:

5 to 8 servings

Cooking method:

Dutch oven

Cooking Temperature:

375 degrees F

Ingredients:

6 cups flour

2 ½ cups yogurt, plain

½ cup water

2 tablespoons sugar

2 tablespoons salt

1 tablespoon olive oil

2 tablespoons yeast

2 tablespoons honey

Directions:

1. Warm water to lukewarm in a saucepan and add yeast, yogurt, honey, salt, sugar and oil.

2. Remove from heat and add flour slowly, kneading into a dough.
3. Place dough in a bowl and let it rise for an hour.
4. Punch the dough down.
5. Form it into a loaf and let it rise again for another hour.
6. Prepare Dutch oven for cooking at 350 degrees F.
7. Place bread in oven and cook for 45 minutes to an hour, or until dough forms a crispy crust and starts to brown.
8. Remove bread from oven and let cool before serving.

Egg And Sausage Casserole

Serving size:

8 to 10 servings

Cooking method:

Dutch oven

Cooking Temperature:

350 degrees F

Ingredients:

10 slices of bread

3 pounds of sausage, cooked and crumbled

3 cups whole milk

10 eggs

½ cup mushrooms, sliced

2 cups cheddar cheese, grated

2 tablespoons olive oil

2 tablespoons mustard

1 teaspoon salt

1 teaspoon black pepper

Directions:

1. Coat inside of Dutch oven with olive oil.
2. Break bread into pieces and add to the bottom of the Dutch oven.
3. Add eggs, milk, mustard, salt and pepper to a bowl and beat until combined.
4. Stir in sausage and mushrooms.
5. Pour egg mixture over the bread pieces in the bottom of the oven.
6. Place lid on Dutch oven and cook at 350 degrees F for 30 minutes.

7. Remove lid and sprinkle cheese on top.
8. Cook for an additional 15 minutes, or until cheese melts and starts to brown.
9. Serve warm.

Fried Eggs

Serving size:

As many as you want

Cooking method:

Dutch oven

Cooking Temperature:

350 degrees F

Ingredients:

Eggs

1 teaspoon extra-virgin olive oil

Salt and pepper, to taste

Directions:

1. Flip the Dutch oven lid upside down and place it in the hot embers of the campfire.
2. Give it a few minutes to heat up and add the olive oil to the lid.
3. Crack the eggs and dump the contents of the egg onto the lid.
4. As long as the embers are hot enough, the eggs will fry just like they would in a skillet.
5. Season with salt and pepper and serve warm.

Ground Beef Goulash

Serving size:

8 to 12 servings

Cooking method:

Dutch oven

Cooking Temperature:

350 degrees F

Ingredients:

3 pounds ground beef

2 medium onions, chopped

2 26-ounce cans of whole tomatoes

2 tablespoons garlic powder

1 tablespoon oregano

1 teaspoon parsley, chopped

Salt and pepper, to taste

2 tablespoons extra virgin olive oil

Directions:
1. Place Dutch oven in hot coals and let it heat up.
2. Add oil to Dutch oven.
3. Add onions and garlic to oven and cook until onions start to turn clear.
4. Add hamburger and cook until it starts to brown.
5. Add tomatoes and chop into pieces with a spatula.
6. Add seasonings and stir in.
7. Cook for 30 minutes, or until hot.
8. Serve with rice or wrap in tortillas and eat like a burrito.

Meatloaf

Serving size:

6 to 8 servings

Cooking method:

Dutch oven

Cooking Temperature:

350 degrees F

Ingredients:

3 pounds ground beef

3 eggs

1 medium onion, chopped

1 cup quick oats

5 tablespoons onion powder

1 tablespoon salt

¼ tablespoon marjoram

½ cup ketchup

Directions:

1. Combine all ingredients except ketchup in a bowl and knead together.
2. Place in a metal casserole pan and form into the shape of a loaf.
3. Prepare Dutch oven for cooking at 350 degrees F.
4. Place casserole pan in Dutch oven. Use stones to keep the pan from coming in contact with the bottom of the oven.
5. Cook with lid on for 30 minutes.
6. Remove lid and spread ketchup across top of meatloaf.
7. Replace lid and cook for another half hour to 45 minutes.
8. Remove the casserole tin from the oven and let cool for 10 minutes before cutting and serving meatloaf.

Onion Rings

Serving size:

8 to 12 servings

Cooking method:

Dutch oven

Cooking Temperature:

400 degrees F

Ingredients:

3 large onions, cut into rings

3 cups buttermilk

3 cups flour

½ teaspoon paprika

1 teaspoon salt

½ teaspoon black pepper

3 cups corn oil, for frying

Directions:

1. Prepare Dutch oven for cooking.
2. Add cooking oil to Dutch oven.
3. Cut onions into rings.
4. Combine buttermilk, flour, paprika, salt and black pepper and whisk until smooth. You want a runny batter. Add more buttermilk if it's too thick or more flour if it's too thin.
5. Dip the onion rings into the batter and drop in the hot oil. The onion rings should start to fry. If not, you've got to raise the temperature of the Dutch oven by placing more coals beneath it.
6. Fry onion rings for a couple minutes until golden brown.
7. Remove from oil and drain.
8. Serve warm.

Pesto Chicken

Serving size:

8 to 12 servings

Cooking method:

Dutch oven

Cooking Temperature:

350 degrees F

Ingredients:

8 boneless, skinless chicken breasts

1 cup mozzarella cheese

Pesto Ingredients:

1 cup basil leaves

1 clove of garlic

½ cup grated Pecorino cheese

½ cup extra virgin olive oil

½ cup walnuts, chopped

A pinch of salt

A dash of pepper

Directions:

1. Blend all of the pesto ingredients in a food processor to make the pesto sauce. This can be done ahead of time, so you don't have to bring a blender along. Alternatively, you can buy premade pesto sauce.
2. Spread half of the pesto across the bottom of the Dutch oven.
3. Place the chicken in the Dutch oven.
4. Spread the remaining pesto on top of the chicken.
5. Place the Dutch oven in the coals of the fire.
6. Place the lid on it and place coals on top of the lid.
7. Cook for a half hour.

8. Remove lid and sprinkle cheese across the top of the chicken.
9. Replace the lid and cook for another 10 to 15 minutes, or until chicken is done and cheese starts to brown.
10. Let cool for a few minutes and serve warm.

Pizza Rolls

Serving size:

8 servings

Cooking method:

Dutch oven

Cooking Temperature:

400 degrees F

Ingredients:

1 can of instant crescent rolls

1 package sausage

1 package sliced pepperoni

½ cup tomato sauce

1 cup shredded mozzarella cheese

Directions:

1. Roll out each of the croissants.
2. Spread tomato sauce across the inside.
3. Stuff with sausage, pepperoni and cheese.
4. Roll up so the pepperoni, sausage and cheese are on the inside.
5. Place in a greased Dutch oven and place the Dutch oven in the fire.
6. Place the lid on the Dutch oven and add coals to bring Dutch oven to proper temperature.
7. Cook for 10 to 20 minutes, or until the cheese inside the pizza roll is melted and the dough is cooked to a golden brown color.
8. Let cool for 8 to 10 minutes and serve warm.

Pot Roast

Serving size:

8 to 12 servings

Cooking method:

Dutch oven

Cooking Temperature:

350 degrees F

Ingredients:

1 pot roast, 3 to 4 pounds

10 new potatoes, halved

5 carrots, peeled and cut into coins

1 onion, chopped

1 cup fresh mushrooms, sliced

4 tablespoons extra virgin olive oil

1 tablespoon salt

1 tablespoon pepper

1 cup water

2 tablespoons Worcestershire sauce

Directions:
1. Rub oil into the roast.
2. Prepare Dutch oven for cooking at 350 degrees F.
3. Place roast in Dutch oven and cook until browned on all sides.
4. Remove meat and add all ingredients to the Dutch oven and stir.
5. Return roast to the oven.
6. Put lid on oven and cook for 3 to 4 hours, or until roast is cooked to your liking.

www.ingramcontent.com/pod-product-compliance
Lightning Source LLC
Chambersburg PA
CBHW071434070526
44578CB00001B/97